I0156787

CUP IT UP!
Team Building with Cups

Other resources from Chris Cavert, Ed.D

For the eBook version and other teambuilding resources please visit FUNdoing.com

Portable Teambuilding Activities:
Games, Initiative, and Team Challenges for Any Space

Affordable Portables:
Initiative Activities and Problem Solving Elements

Games for Teachers:
Activities That Promote Pro-Social Learning
with Laurie Frank

50 Ways to Use Your Noodle:
Loads of Land Games Using Foam Pool Noodle Toys
with Sam Sikes

(See more of Chris' titles at his FUNdoing.com
website.)

Other resources from
Barry W Thompson

www.WhenPeoplePlay.com (Teambuilding Videos and Game Resources)

YouTube Channel:
https://www.youtube.com/c/WhenPeoplePlay   [W]

Instagram: @whenpeopleplay

If you want the latest updates to all things go here:
linktr.ee/whenpeopleplay

Sales and Distribution

Hard Copy Sales & Distribution - Contact Barry through: www.WhenPeoplePlay.com or barry@whenpeopleplay.com

Digital Download - Go to www.FUNdoing.com

1st Edition - Digital & Hard Copy (c) 2017, Thompson & Cavert
All Rights Reserved

Cover Graphic by Barry W. Thompson
Photos by Chris Cavert & Barry W. Thompson

Gratitudes

We are so grateful for all of the help we had on this project.

Our biggest thanks goes out to Group Dynamix (GroupDynamix.com) for all the "space" they gave us to work out our activities, and to the GDX staff who tried and tweaked them over the years. You are the BEST!!

Thanks to our reviewers:
Jennifer Steinmetz, Greg Huber, Katie Martin, Holly Scherer and Ben Vanderzyden.
The changes you inspired certainly made the book better!!

Thanks to our editors:
Linda A. Williams and Steve Creighton
We truly appreciate your final touches!!

To our family and friends. You inspire us each and every day!!

Finally...to you,
the team builder,
the change agent,
the thought leader,
the game master,
the motivator,
the inspirer.

Cup It Up friends and do good work!!

BONUS MATERIAL! If you would like an easy download of the instructions and questions to the the activities in this book, then please visit: http://www.fundoing.com/resources.html

or

As a thank you, we want to give some bonuses for buying the paperback. To get your bonuses please visit www.whenpeopleplay.com/cup-bonus

Table of Contents

ACTIVITIES

Activity Objective: As quickly and efficiently as possible, without "cupollapse", the group is challenged to build, and then un-build, a cup stack pyramid. Each group member is responsible for adding and then subtracting one or more cups.

Activity Objective: In this timed activity, partners or small teams work together to flip over a cup that is poised atop a bandana, fill it with an orb (e.g., tennis ball) and then stand the cup back up. All of this is done by holding and manipulating the edges of the bandana.

Activity Objective: Blindfolded builders, with cup in hand, are guided into a building area to build, or build upon, cup towers. Each stacked cup compounds in points. The overall team (or each team's) objective is to obtain the most points within the time allowed.

Activity Objective: Small groups write as many questions as they can on their cup. After the cups are passed around from group to group, the goal is to have the least amount of check marks - being the group with the most unique life experiences at the time.

Activity Objective: Match all the numbered cups with the numbered spots - only two cups can be moved at a time.

Activity Objective: As a group, line up all the cup sets available in sequential order as quickly as possible.

Activity Objective: Using cups - in a particular way - the group is challenged to move the material provided (e.g., tennis balls) from one point to another with as little "loss" as possible.

Activity Objective: Be the first team to bounce a ping pong ball into each of the 12 cups provided - making each cup float above the one below.

Activity Objective: Slalom a ping pong ball through a series of cups from one end of the table to the other as quickly as possible using only lung power.

Activity Objective: Build the tallest cup pyramid starting with the top level of a single cup.

Activity Objective: First, how many cups can be stacked end to end supported by the team? When stacked and supported, how many times can the group rotate the stack like a waterwheel to get as many ping pong balls into the bucket?

Discussions with Cups

Activity Objective: At the beginning of the program: Get to know others and ultimately remember what fills each person's cup.

Activity Objective: At the end of a program: Leave everyone with a wide variety of positive feedback.

Introduction

Since the creation of the Red Plastic Cup in the 1970s, it's popularity with hundreds of thousands of people and dozens of cultures all over America grew with gatherings like birthday parties, church functions, holidays and picnics with family and friends. Since it was cheap and easily accessible, this famous Red Cup became a common sight at sporting events, inspired the lyrics to a popular country song (Red Solo Cup by Toby Keith), and caused many a college student to miss morning classes following late-night games of beer pong.

Beyond the fun and interactive experiences we know you will have with these 12 new team building activities, our hope is that you use the "Cup" as a metaphor for life. Discussions can evolve from:

- What fills your cup? What helps you learn and grow?
- What fills up the cups of the people you work with? What helps them learn and grow?
- What will you raise your cup to? What will they raise their cup to?

The "cuptivities" in this book were designed to promote conversations and questions about keeping our cup filled with knowledge and awareness. Most of us have struggled with giving - or pouring out - too much of ourselves for the benefit of others resulting in the neglect of ourselves. If you are constantly pouring for - or serving - everyone else without refreshing yourself, it won't be long before your energy and joy are depleted. In order to most effectively give, give back, facilitate, lead, or run a team, take care of yourself and "fill your cup" too.

Thank you for choosing this book to supplement your wealth of team building activities. We hope that you will continue to be inspired by the Red Plastic Cup. Not only for parties and play but also to encourage, to teach and to help others grow and learn for themselves.

Our hope is that you enjoy the Cup lessons and camaraderie as much as we have.

Chris Cavert and Barry [W] Thompson

Cupology

Over the last two years (and even longer for Barry), we have been trying out all sorts of cups for the activities in this book. Now, we could share all of our research with you, of course, but we would rather skip right to the good stuff.

CUPS: We prefer the 18-ounce Solo® squared bottom cup for all the activities in the book; however, just about any other plastic party-style cup will work. We are especially partial to the brands that provide a variety of colors - they are lots of fun. One major discovery in our research was that "other" party-style cups don't seem to last as long - their construction is a bit thinner.

With that said, if you wanted to invest in a sturdier plastic cup (the dishwasher safe variety) then go for it. We like the party-style price, weight, and portability.

Speaking of sturdy cups, if you are familiar with Speed Stacks® Sport Stacking cups, they work great, as well (for more information go to: speedstacks.com). If you have access to a number of Speed Stacks® sets you now have more to do with them.

CUP VOCABULARY:

Open Cup The cup is in a position where the open end is up.

Closed Cup The cup is in a position where the open end is down.

Nested Cups, Closed

Nested Cups, Open

Activity Formatting Information

The following is related to how we've formatted each activity. Some of the headings will be familiar to you, while others might be new. This will give you an understanding about how we have organized the information we find important.

NOTE: The activities in this book are organized in alphabetical order, with the exception of "Cup Ups" found at the end of the book. You have the freedom (as you always do) to program the activities where they will best fit the needs of your groups.

Activity Name: This is the name for the activity based on the context (about cups) of this book. As many of us know, there are thousands of activities out there suitable for team building and adventure education work. Some (if not most) of these activities are identified by activity objective, just a different name (and probably using different equipment). We've named the Cup activities here in the way that works for us. THIS IS A GOOD THING! Roll with it. Embrace it. Change the name if a different one fits your programming better. It's all good.

Some historical context is included under the name for some of the activities. If you know something about an activity we failed to mention, please let us know.

We will be happy to add to the history or correct any mistakes. The activities that do not include a historical perspective at this time have been developed by us. Now, this does not mean these entries are completely novel. There could be someone, somewhere with the same idea. If you are one of those "someones" please let us know, and we'll share the glory. As we've often heard from Karl Rohnke (who heard it from someone else) within the context of adventure education, "A good idea doesn't care who has it."

Activity Objective: This is the overall goal of the activity itself. For example, move tennis balls to the container at the far end of the room with the least number of drops. Then, of course, you set up the guidelines (or restrictions) as to how they are allowed to meet the objectives. Using a competitive analogy, the activity objective of playing soccer is to score goals and win the game, adhering to the rules of play. To make the clear contrast, an Activity Objective is about the activity. A Facilitated Objective (up next) is about the potential experiential and learning outcomes that are possible from the activity.

Facilitated Objective: This section includes a variety of behaviors and concepts that could be explored through the activity and debrief. While there are "typical" behaviors and concepts that present themselves during these activities, facilitators should choose an approach that relates to working on and moving toward accomplishing the particular goals/objectives the group brings with them to a program.

For example, if a group wants to improve communication skills/behaviors, Material Movers can be used to encourage talking (i.e., communicating). This activity requires verbal communication during the planning stage, as well as during problem solving situations that will no doubt present themselves. The behaviors and concepts listed for each activity are based on our personal experiences with the activities and may not always present themselves with every group. It will depend on the people in the group and their level of development. (On a personal note, Chris has a working theory that any adventure-based activity could potentially touch upon any social behavior depending on how the activity is presented and talked about before, during and afterward - but that's another book.)

Keep in mind that the behaviors and concepts listed in this book are fairly subjective, interpreted through different personal lenses and contexts. During teambuilding and adventure education experiences we talk about concepts like "trust," "leadership" and "communication." The idea is to explore what these concepts mean to the individuals in the group and how they understand them within that context in order to move forward with the tasks presented. Through the individuals' shared experiences with the behaviors and concepts, each person then has the opportunity to stick with the behaviors he or she regularly elicits or change behaviors based on new information. Please know that the behaviors and concepts shared within each activity are a starting point and not exhaustive. They are meant to stimulate awareness about what the activities can bring about in a group. They are part of the "education" in adventure education.

Needs: This section lists and details the equipment needed for the activity. Of course, feel free to change the equipment based on your available resources and programming needs (and your curiosity).

Numbers: Based on our experiences with the activities we suggest a range of group participants, suggesting numbers we have believe keep people interested and engaged. Please feel free to try group sizes outside the ranges (and do let us know how it works out - we can learn from you).

Time: In this section, we include a fair range of time you might want to program for the particular activity. In some cases, more time will be needed for particular activities if your group is engaged in the process or is ready for some deep conversation. As always, keep an eye on your group, noticing behaviors that might indicate the need to pause and check in, reflect a bit before continuing or stop the activity and move on to another educational experience.

Procedure: This is the information for setting up the activity and the guidelines for play. The procedures we share are basically one way to present the experience. As always, feel free to adjust the setup and guidelines in order to meet the needs of your group.

Safety: This section describes particular safety concerns (physical and/or emotional) related to the activity - if we have experienced or heard about them. These points will certainly not be exhaustive. Be mindful of your group and step in for safety reasons if necessary. On that note, here are a couple bits of information to consider. Chris' friend Paul recently tweeted, "In our business 'safe' is a four-letter word." And, Karl Rohnke is well known for sharing: "If it's completely safe, it's no longer an adventure." Balance this advice with your experience. Work within a safety spectrum with which you are comfortable and your program procedures dictate.

Facilitation: This section includes some of the ways in which we facilitate the activity. Here are the tips and tricks, as well as some friendly advice based on our experience. Feel free to adjust your approach in a way that better suits your group's needs and their goals. One of the aspects of team building and adventure education programs we truly appreciate is the flexibility within the methods. As we've come to know, it's not about the activities themselves. The learning and growth come from what happens during the activities.

Observations/Questions: This section has two
distinct purposes. Reviewing the list of questions
before you deliver the activity (even during your
programming process) will give you an idea of the
possible outcomes of the activity experience - the
concepts and behaviors that might occur during the
activity. In other words, things you might observe
during the groups experience with the particular
activity. Newer facilitators can find the observation
prompts useful when preparing for programs.

After a program, for review or processing discussions,
you can use the questions to open up conversations
about the particular Facilitated Objectives listed for
the activity. Depending on the objectives of the group
you may use one or two of the Facilitated Objectives
questions (each set is directly related to one of the
Facilitated Objectives listed for the activity) or direct
the discussion using different questions that are more
relevant to the experience of the group.

As always, we encourage you not to limit your
observations and questions to these suggestions; they
are intended to be starting points for possible
discussion.

Variations: This section includes additional ideas for
setting up and/or presenting the activity. When

programming for a variety of groups, we find it useful to have ways to modify the activities in order to better meet the needs of different groups. There are some variations that, in our opinion, make the activity easier or more challenging. Please take them "with a grain of salt" because one group might not respond to a variation the same way as another. When it comes to changing something, listen to your gut! It's usually right.

On this "Variations" note, we love new ideas, so if you design something new for any of these activities, please let us know so we can share.

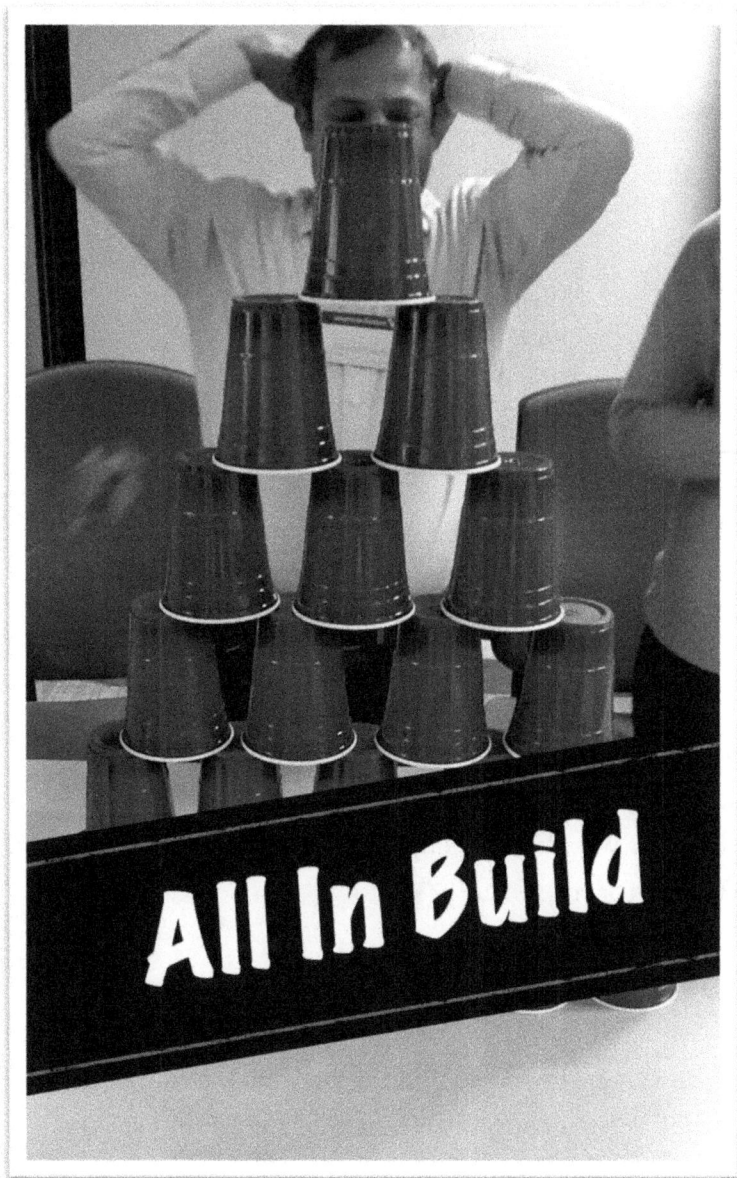

All In Build

All In Build

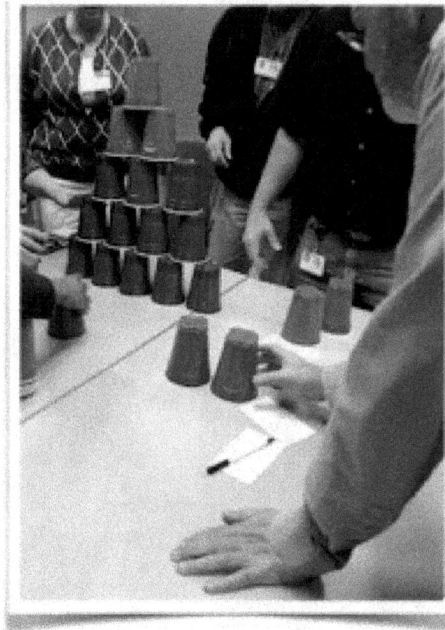

Cup stacking has been around since the invention of the cup. Why make a cup tower by yourself - add some friends for more fun!

Activity Objective: As quickly and efficiently as possible, without "cupollapse", the group is challenged to build, and then un-build, a cup stack pyramid. Each player in the group is responsible for adding and then subtracting one or more cups.

Facilitated Objective:
1. Planning and implementation of the plan.
2. Exploring leadership behaviors.
3. Defining roles and responsibilities.
4. Being chosen for a task or choosing for yourself.
5. The importance of focus.
6. The details surrounding project management.
7. Working on behaviors related to crisis management.
8. Exploring and practicing goal-setting.

Needs Per Group:
- 15 cups (for a 5-cup base pyramid) or,
- 21 cups (for a 6-base pyramid), or more for a higher tower
- 1 solid building area (e.g., table top or tile floor)
- 1 timing device

NOTE: Adding more cups to the build will extend the time and the challenge level of the activity.

Numbers: 10 to 12 players in a group. Multiple groups can play at once.

Time: 15 to 20 minutes.

Procedure: The "Build" challenge in this activity is defined as constructing a pyramid (like the graphic below) and then deconstructing it (i.e., taking it down) as quickly as possible. Determine how many cups you want to use for the build, keeping in mind that adding more cups means more challenge. You may want to start with fewer cups and add more later to increase the complexity of the task. Use the graphic below to determine the number of cups you will need for your desired level of difficulty.

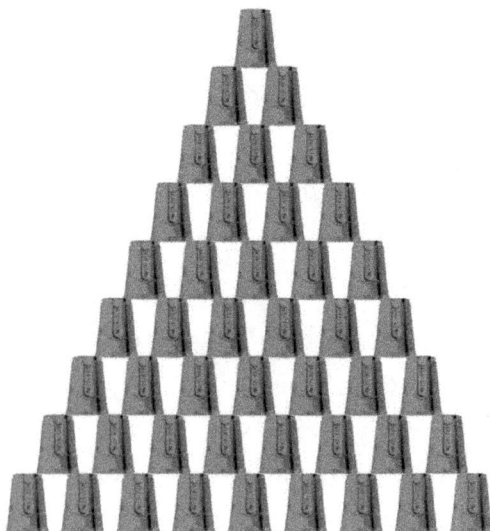

1 Level = 1 Cup

2 Levels = 3 Cups

3 Levels = 6 Cups

4 Levels = 10 Cups

5 Levels = 15 Cups

6 Levels = 21 Cups

7 Levels = 28 Cups

8 Levels = 36 Cups

9 Levels = 45 Cups

Explain to the group that each player must add at least one cup to, and take away at least one cup from, the pyramid during each build attempt. When a player is given (or takes) more than one cup for a build, this player may not add or remove those cups one right after the other. In other words, players must take turns. For example, if Philip places a cup onto the pyramid, someone else must place the next cup onto the pyramid before Phillip is allowed to add another cup. The same will be true for taking away cups during deconstruction.

After all the cups for the impending build are distributed (one or more for each player depending on the number of cups in the build), each player must set his/her cup(s) down, in the open position, near the building area. Next, share the Rules of the activity (below) with the group and then give them some time to plan and practice their building process before the timed attempt. (Choose the amount of planning time they should have based on their goals and desired outcomes).

Rules:
- Time for the build starts when the timer says, "Go!" (The time can be kept by the facilitator or a group member depending on the objectives of the group.)
- All the cups provided must be used in the pyramid.

- Each row of the pyramid has one more cup than the row above it and the top row of the pyramid is comprised of one cup.
- Each player is responsible for placing the cup or cups he/she was given into the build, one at a time.
- Each player is responsible for removing the same number of cups as he/she placed (not necessarily the same cups).
- The time stops when all the cups provided are standing in one nested stack in the closed position.

Depending on programming objectives, give the group a number of attempts at each build to improve their process (e.g., time, efficiency). Add more cups to increase the complexity of the task and/or use one or more of the variations below to see how players adjust to the changes (if this idea fits into your program objectives). You could also introduce goal-setting, the group setting a particular completion time, to motivate results.

Safety: At this point we have not experienced any physical safety issues related to All In Build. Be mindful of any safety issues related to the location you set up this activity and make your group aware of potential situations to avoid.

Facilitation: We've run All In Build a couple of different ways - single group challenge builds (as described above) and builds involving multiple teams. For single group challenges, we like to start with a small tower, one or two cups per player. We have the group set a "time-to-beat" (TTB) goal. Once they reach their goal, we increase the challenge level by adding more cups at the start of each build and setting a new TTB goal. Goal setting and timing the builds for single groups provide the motivation for additional challenges.

When running (respectfully) competitive All In Builds we typically offer at least two heats (there has to be at least one re-match!). And, the cups start out in one nested stack in the closed position near the building area for each team.

Teams, made up of about seven or eight players, are challenged to build a 21 cup (six level) pyramid. After a three minute planning and practice session the first heat can begin. When "GO!" is called, players from each team may only take one cup at a time off of their stack and place it onto the build. A player may not take another cup off of their nested stack until every other player has taken a cup off the stack and placed it onto the build. And, progressively, a player may not take a third cup until every other player has placed a second cup onto the build. The same requirements are in place for deconstruction - ending up with one nested cup stack on the building area in the closed position. Places are given (first, second, third, etc.) based on when a team finishes their build process.

During heat two (after a three-minute planning and practice session) the start is the same - a nested cup stack starts in the closed position on near the building area. However, the requirements change slightly. Each participant must use the same hand during construction and then use the opposite hand for deconstruction. This change in the process adds a nice complexity to the second heat. If you run a third heat, add a different rule to spice it up.

As always, feel free to adjust any of the activity conditions to meet group needs.

Observations/Questions:

1. Planning and implementation of the plan:
   A. How would you describe a smooth productive planning session?
   B. Share a story about a productive planning session you have been a part of in the past.
   C. How would you compare your recent planning session for this activity to a past planning session - whether it was a positive or negative experience in the past?
   D. If you did have a plan in place for this last activity, how was its overall implementation?
   E. What went "according to plan" and what did not?
   F. What was missing from the implementation of the plan?
   G. What do you want to remember for the next planning session?

2. Exploring leadership behaviors:
   A. Describe the leadership behaviors you noticed during the activity.
   B. Which ones did you like and which ones would you like to see changed?
   C. What are some of the positive and negative aspects of leadership you've experienced in the past?

3. Defining roles and responsibilities:

   A. What role(s) did you play during the activity? Were you "assigned" this role, or is it one that you chose?

   B. Did you "like" the role you had? Why? Why Not?

   C. Did your role change during the activity? Why did this happen?

4. Being chosen for a task or choosing for yourself:

   A. What other roles were present during the activity?

   B. Were they helpful or unhelpful roles?

   C. What roles, the good and not-so-good, were missing?

5. The importance of focus:

   A. How many of you found yourself being distracted during the activity - being drawn away from the specific task at hand?

   B. Why do you think this happened to you?

   C. What helps you keep your focus during an important task?

   D. What tools/behaviors can we use to help us keep focus?

6. The details surrounding project management:
   A. How would you define "project management?"
   B. What "parts" are involved in project management?
   C. What parts did you manage during this last activity?
   D. How were these parts related to your success?
   E. What parts were missing and how did they impact your success?

7. Working on behaviors related to crisis management:
   A. Did you (or the group) find yourself in crisis during the activity?
   B. What did this crisis look like and sound like?
   C. What did you do (the behaviors that showed up for you) specifically when you found yourself in crisis?
   D. Looking back on the crisis moment(s), is there anything you would do differently?
   E. Are there any other choices you would have made?

8. Exploring and practicing goal-setting:
   A. When you were asked to set some goals for yourself or as a group, what did you notice

about the process?

B. Is setting goals useful for you? Why or why not?

C. Give an example of when goal setting has been useful to you?

D. Share a story about a goal setting experience you've had the past - how did it turn out?

E. What do we know about goal setting?

F. What do we want to remember about goal setting in the future?

Variations:

- Add one or more of these rules to the process: Cups may not be touched until "GO!" is called. If a player has more than one cup to add to the build, they can't be placed onto the build consecutively. If a player has more than one cup to add and then take away from the build, he/she cannot place them together in the final nested stack.

- Make the activity more structured by numbering (or lettering) the bottom (outside) of the cups - if you have cups ready for Line Em' Up, use them for All In. With numbered/lettered cups, you can present different building requirements (e.g., an odd number cannot be next to an even number or numbers can't be next to each other in sequence).

- Using numbered/lettered cups, start the build with all the cups in a nested stack (closed) from highest number/letter at the bottom of the stack to number one/letter A at the top of the stack. Each player is assigned, and is responsible for, one to three non-sequential numbered/lettered cups. Players can only touch their assigned numbered/lettered cups. To spice this one up even more, randomly nest the cups together for the start and require the cups in the build to be in sequential order. (Crazy! We know!)

- Each player can only use one hand during the build - maybe the dominant hand to build up and the non-dominant for the take down.

- For a leadership focus, all but two players have their eyes closed. The two with their eyes open guide the build up and take down. (We recommend the smaller pyramid builds for this one.)

- Deal out number index cards - each card matches a number on one of the cups provided (or numbered spots like the ones used in Cup Switch). When time starts, players can flip over and look at their index cards/spots to see the cups in which they have to place in the stack. (Thanks Greg H.)

- Use math sums or build words at each level of the pyramid. Have the numbers in each row equal a number like 36 - you'll need to provide the numbered cups to make this work. Require each row to be a different word or the whole pyramid makes a sentence.

(Thanks Ben V.)

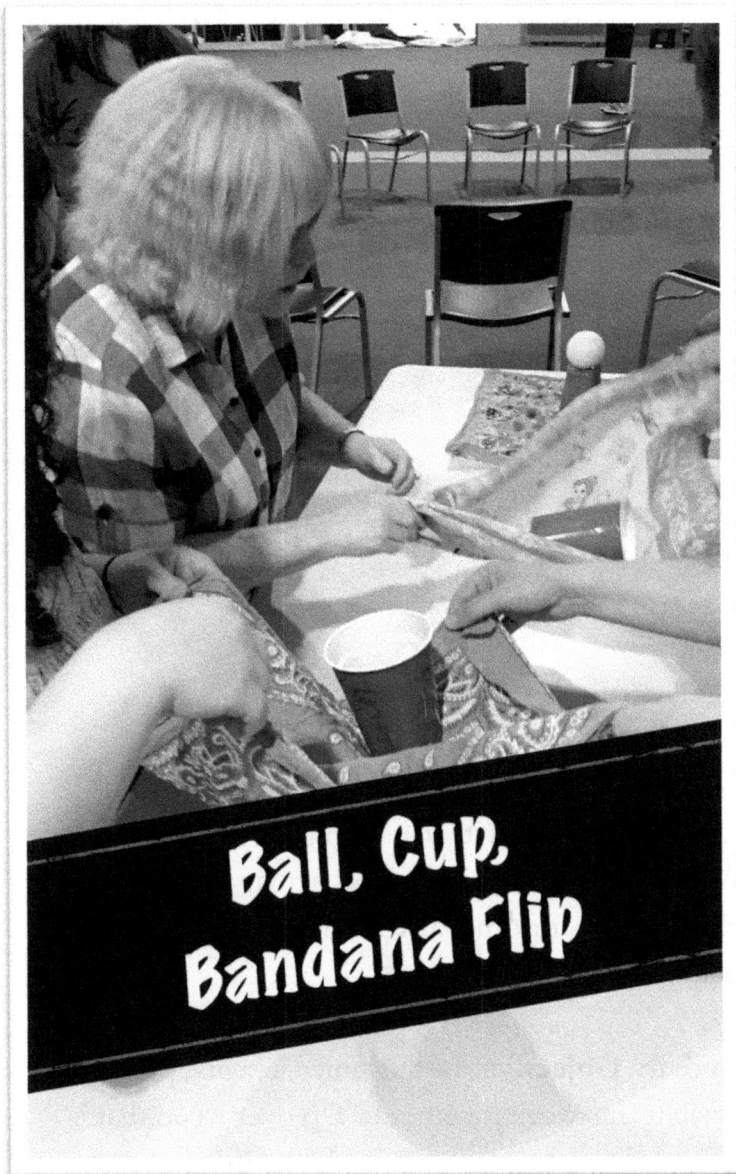

Ball, Cup,
Bandana Flip

Ball, Cup, Bandana Flip
(a.k.a., Flipping Out)

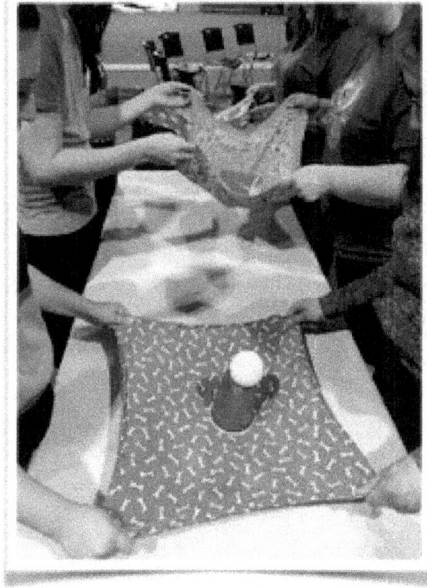

Credit for this activity variation goes to Tom Heck. After seeing his version of this activity the marble was changed out for other "orb" choices (e.g., a tennis ball).

Activity Objective: In this timed activity, partners or small teams work together to flip over a cup that is poised atop a bandana, fill it with an orb and then stand it back up. All of this is done by holding and manipulating the edges of the bandana.

Facilitated Objective:

1. Exploring behaviors related to communication.
2. Implementation of the plan and adapting to changes:
3. Collaboration and cooperation (and distinguishing between the two).
4. Persistence.
5. Overcoming failure.
6. Celebrating success.

Needs Per Group:

- 1 bandana
- 1 cup
- 1 orb (e.g., ping pong ball, tennis ball, bouncy ball - bigger than a tennis ball)

Numbers: Two to four players per group. Multiple groups can play at once. This one can be played with 50, or more, people if you have the gear.

Time: 10 to 15 minutes.

Procedure: Divide your entire group into smaller groups of two to four players. Give each small group one bandana, one cup, and one orb (we'll use a ping-pong ball for this description). To start, have each small group lay out their bandana flat on a hard surface (e.g., floor or table). Have them place the cup on the bandana in the closed position. Finally, have them place the ping-pong ball on the bottom part of the cup as shown in the first graphic below. This is the "start" position.

From this start position, the goal of the activity is to get the ping-pong ball inside the cup ending with the cup in the open position on top of the bandana - this is called a "flip". Players may only hold the bandana by the edges. They may not touch the cup or the ping-pong ball in any way during the activity - not even through the bandana. If the ping-pong ball and/or cup falls off of the bandana they must reset the equipment back into the start position.

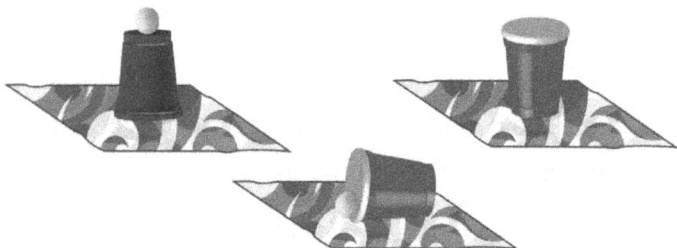

Give the groups a couple of minutes to practice the flip process. After practicing, the challenge for each small group is to see how many times they can accomplish the flip in five minutes. After each successful flip the bandana is placed back on the floor/table. The cup and ping-pong ball are then reset to the start position before the next flip attempt can take place. Have each group keep their own score. After five minutes record all small group scores and add them together. Challenge the group, as a whole, to improve upon this total score.

Play two or three five-minute rounds for the best possible "All-Group" score.

Safety: Since we've been facilitating this one, there haven't been any safety issues observed. When needed, make participants aware of any hazards in the surrounding area.

Facilitation: When we program this one we usually gather people together to demonstrate the flip. We also demonstrate how "not" to grab the cup or ping-pong ball. (The flip is not as easy as you think, so be sure to get some practice.)

This highly accessible activity is also a good one for taking a break from standing if the group needs one. It can easily be done sitting around a table.

42

Observations/Questions:

1. Exploring behaviors related to communication:
   A. Describe the communication in your small group as it related problem solving?
   B. What did you hear? What did you not hear?
   C. Was the communication working? Explain?
   D. Could your communication have been better? How so?

2. Implementation of the plan and adapting to changes:
   A. Describe the plan of action you developed during your practice session.
   B. What, if anything, did you have to change about your plan once you got started flipping?
   C. During the course of flipping what adjustments did you need to make in relation to your partner's course of action?
   D. If they changed the plan on you, how did you react?

3. Collaboration and cooperation (and distinguishing between the two):
   A. What do you know about the difference between collaboration and cooperation?
   B. Looking back on the activity were you collaborating or cooperating (or both)?
   C. During the activity, were you comparing and sharing ideas?
   D. Did you agree with the ideas, or disagree? How did you share your opinion?
   E. How were disagreements handled?

4. Persistence:
   A. At any point during the activity did you feel like giving up?
   B. What do you believe is important about persistence?
   C. When might persistence be a bad thing?

5. Overcoming failure:
   A. What (if anything) did you "fail" at during your process?
   B. How does/did this information inform your work together as a group?
   C. Did you try different ideas during your practice session?
   D. Was it easier when there were 2 or 4 people around the bandana?
   E. After hearing all the scores, what did you learn about your overall process?
   F. What did/can you do with this learning?

6. Celebrating success:
   A. If you were given $100 for each successful flip, how would this change the activity for your group?
   B. If each successful flip added a can of food to the local food pantry, how would this change the activity for your group?
   C. Speaking for yourself, do repetitive tasks tend to gain value or lose value over time?
   D. What types of repetitive tasks gain value for you over time?

E. What types of tasks lose value for you over time? Why do you think that is?

F. Were you successful?

G. How do/did you measure your success?

H. Why might it be important to celebrate success?

I. What is a negative outcome of over-celebrating?

Variations:

- Try the flips without talking.

- Use this activity as a race - moving from one point to another. Can the team race the cup with the orb balanced on the cup through an obstacle course without the orb falling off?

- For another race, provide each small group (you might call them teams now) with four different orbs - a marble, a ping-pong ball, a wadded up piece of paper, and a tennis ball. Each team can start with whatever orb they want. After each successful flip, the team must use one of the other orbs. The first team to flip all four orbs wins!

- When working with groups that you want to do more processing with, try this activity without giving them any practice. This variation of the activity allows for discussion towards planning and preparation, changes under pressure, skill development over time, etc.

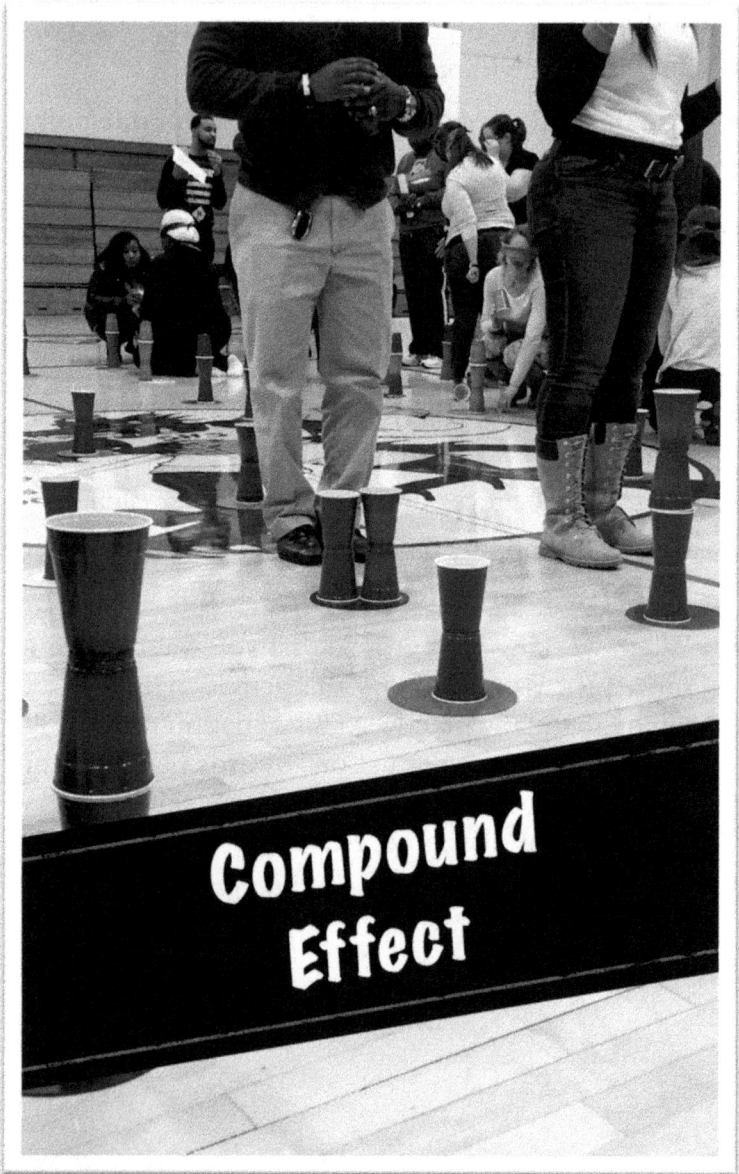

Compound Effect

Compound Effect

This was one of those, "Hey I've got an idea" moments. We discussed the yet-to-be-named activity (now so named) as it morphed four times in our initial five minute brainstorm.

Activity Objective: Blindfolded builders, with cup in hand, are guided into a building area to build, or build upon, cup towers. Each newly stacked cup compounds in points. The team (or each team's) objective is to obtain the most points within the time allowed.

Facilitated Objective:

1. Working with limited resources.
2. Effective communication behaviors.
3. Defining and developing boundaries.
4. Implementation of plans.
5. Building trust.

Needs:

- 1 blindfold (e.g., clean bandana) for each player (NOTE: Using "blindfolds" might not be appropriate - just ask players to close their eyes when building.)
- 4 cups for each player
- 18 to 20 flat objects shared by everyone (e.g., vinyl spots, paper plates, or small wooden boards - cup towers will be built on these flat objects)

If you have a flat tiled or carpeted floor to work with you could also tape out small squares on the floor with masking tape. You are going to set out 18 to 25 flat objects (or tape squares) for a 15x15-foot area marked off by cones or an activity rope. This is called the building area.

Numbers: 15 to 25 players. Multiple groups could play this one at the same time - give all groups the same amount of time to work.

Time: 20 to 30 minutes.

Procedure: First set out your building area (with four cones or a long rope). Evenly distribute the flat objects inside the area. The number of objects you set down within that space is up to you. Consider the following: fewer flat objects will provide more space to walk around (making the activity easier). Obviously, if you place down more flat objects the activity becomes a bit more difficult.

Place the cups you have assigned to the group anywhere outside the boundary area and hand out one blindfold to each player (or simply ask them to close their eyes if they go into the building area with a cup).

The group's objective is to score as many points as possible by building cup towers on the flat objects inside the boundary area. (See the Scoring Table below for the "compound" scoring process.)

Scoring Table

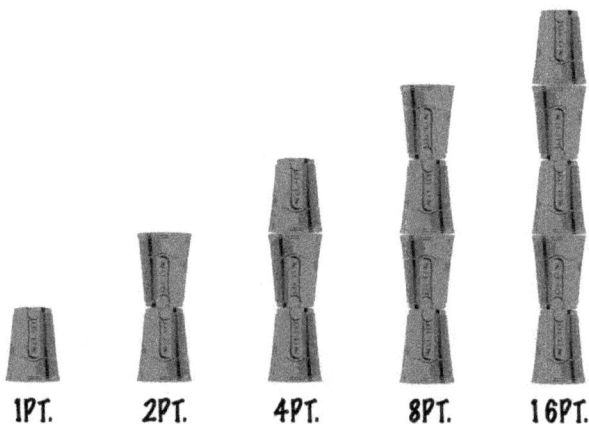

| 1PT. | 2PT. | 4PT. | 8PT. | 16PT. |

Read the guidelines below to the group or give them a copy to read themselves.

Compound Effect Action Guidelines

- Only non-sighted players can be inside the boundary area. There is no limit to the number of players inside the boundary area as long as they are blindfolded.

- You can only bring one cup into the boundary area at a time.

- After placing a cup on one of the flat objects, or another cup, you must exit the building area.

- Sighted participants, standing outside of the building area, are allowed to verbally guide those inside the area.

- Cup towers must be built on the flat objects provided and only one tower can be built on each flat object. Cups must be stacked with like ends together, not nested inside of each other.

- Any cup that touches the floor/carpet/ground inside the building area (not on the flat object) will be removed from the area and may not be used as a building resource.

- Tell your facilitator when you are ready. You will then have 10 minutes to build for points.

Scoring: The first cup placed (in the closed position) on one of the flat objects is worth one point. Any cup that is stacked on top of another cup will be scored in a compound fashion (double the current tower's points). For example, the second cup in the tower will equal two points. The third cup will equal four points. A fourth cup will equal eight points. And so on... (Your facilitator will be happy to give you more details about compound scoring if needed.)

Safety: Blindfolded people tend to bump into each other. Be sure to monitor and watch for any potential problems. Teach the group how to use their hands as bumpers (held up in front of them) to protect each other and ask them to be mindful of the speed they travel at inside the boundary area. Ask the players not to run while inside the boundary area - you know you have to say it!

Facilitation: Depending on your processing objectives (e.g., leadership) and/or the number of players (e.g., 10 to 12), it might be more "experiential" to provide your group with a copy of the bulleted guidelines above.

When facilitating this one there are a couple things you may need to continuously remind the group. Only unsighted players can be in the building area - this means that after a cup is placed this player must exit the building area unsighted as well. Also, if a tower collapses it cannot be rebuilt. In other words, cups cannot be picked up from the floor and used as building resources (these will be taken away by the facilitator).

Observations/Questions:
1. Working with limited resources:
    A. What was it like working around other tower builders to accomplish your task?
    B. Define the boundaries that you created to achieve your task.
    C. What was it like sharing ideas and team strategy?
    D. What was it like to work with limited resources?
    E. What were your resources during the task? How well did you utilize your resources? What could have been better?

2. Effective communication behaviors:
    A. Describe what your communication was like with your team. What worked and what did not work?
    B. What did you observe about the interactions with your partner? What did you see? What did you hear?

3. Defining and developing boundaries:
   A. What boundaries did you set up with your partner?
   B. What boundaries did you set up with your team?
   C. For example, did you just stick to one tower or just work on any tower?

4. Implementation of plans:
   A. Did you come up with a plan or just wing it?
   B. If there was a plan, where did the ideas come from?
   C. When the group was ready to begin the activity, did you know the plan and your part in the plan?
   D. If you didn't really know what was going on, did you say anything? Why do you think people might not speak up if they don't know what's going on?
   E. Once you got started with the plan, did it change over time? If so, why did it have to change?
   F. How do you believe you handle change? Do you handle it well? Not so well? Does it depend? On what?

5. Building trust:
   A. Did you find yourself trusting others around the tower you were working on? Why or why not?
   B. What does it take for others to gain/earn your trust?
   C. What do you do to earn other people's trust?

Variations:

- For higher functioning teams you can deduct points for stepping on flat object in the building area. This opens up a processing discussion on how we deal with boundaries that limit us.

- For some competition, divide the groups into teams. Give each team a different color cup or use different colored flat objects. The team with the most points wins. If you knock over another team's tower, those points go against your team's score. For example, a red cup team member knocks over a tower of three from the blue team. Four points will be deducted from the red cup team.

- Place a plastic tub full of cups in the middle of the building area. Require every blindfolded player to obtain the cup he/she needs to build with from the tub. This variation does add a bit more time to the overall process, but requires all players to move through more of the building area.

- Adjusting the number of flat objects or cups will change the dynamics of the activity. For example, less flat objects may lead to building taller towers - increasing the risk for collapse and losing resources (cups). Providing fewer cups may lead to more planning around how the cups will be used - shorter towers can be safer.

- Expanding the building area plays better with groups of 26 to 50 players.

- Make the flat object building areas more challenging. For example, place flat objects right next to each other, place a flat object on a milk crate or under a table, etc.
(Thanks to Ben V.)

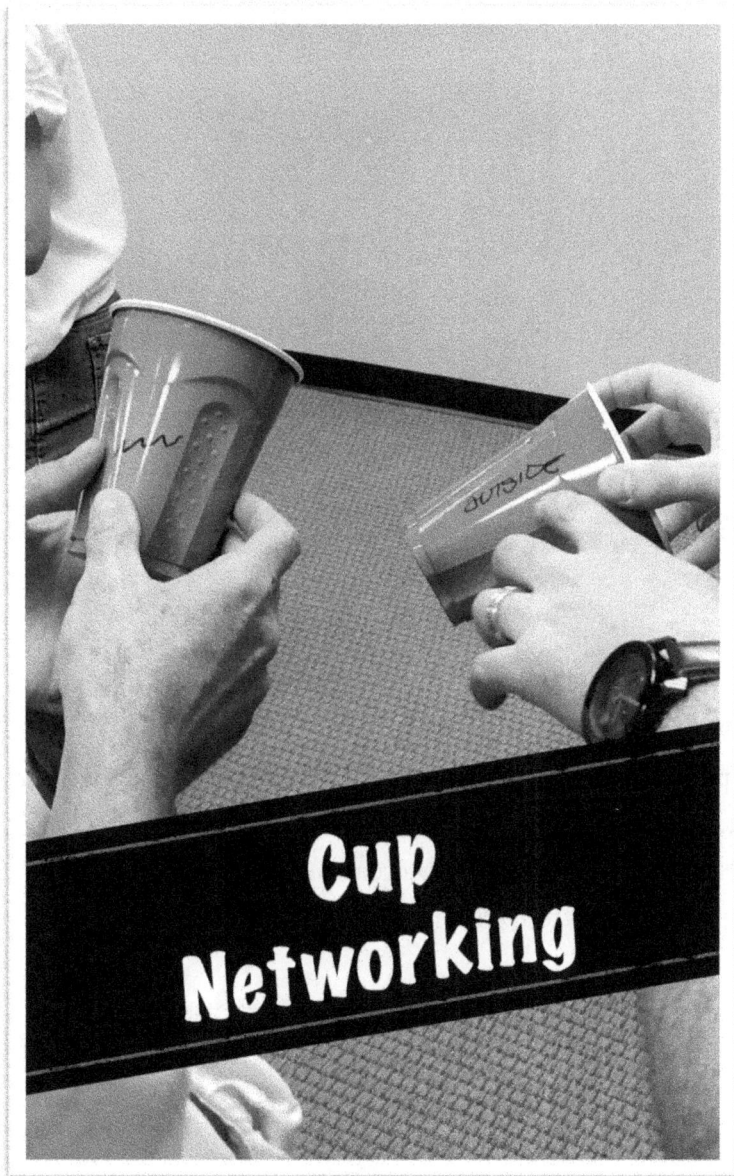

Cup
Networking

Cup Networking

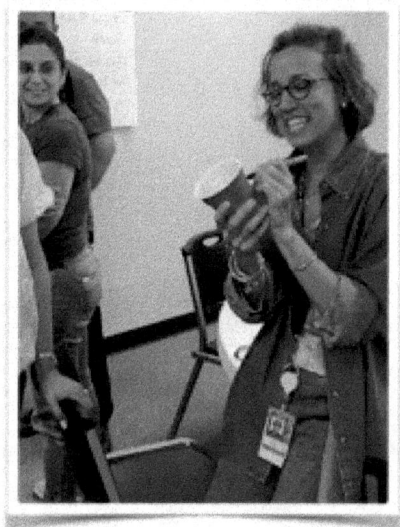

This one was inspired by the activity Human Bingo where players collect signatures on their "Bingo" card (piece of paper) for different achievements reached, or experiences had, by others in the group. For Cup Networking, each group creates their own questions instead of getting them from the facilitator.

Activity Objective: Small groups write as many questions as they can on their cup. After the cups are passed around from group-to-group, the goal is to have the least amount of check marks - being the group with the most unique life experiences at the time.

Facilitated Objective:
1. Discovering commonalities.
2. Building relationships.
3. Building trust.
4. Finding the fun.

Needs Per Group:

• 1 cup

• 1 permanent marker

Have extra cups and markers available for backup.

Numbers: Four to eight players per group. At least four groups will be needed for this one. Plays well with up to 60 participants (divided into at least seven groups).

Time: 20 to 30 minutes.

Procedure: Have everyone gather in a circle, then divide the circle into small groups of four to eight players. The small groups should be arranged together in circle formation, as well, like numbers on a clock (the center of the clock is the center point of the original large circle). The purpose of the clock formation is so that the cups can be passed in

60

a specified fashion later. Give one cup and one permanent marker to each small group. The objective is to have every player in the small group write one unique "Yes" or "No" question on their cup. For example, "Do you like to ride motorcycles?" Or, "Do you know a celebrity?" Each question must be true for the person who writes it on the cup.

When facilitating, ask the players not to write questions that are too common, like, "Have you ever worn shoes?" Everyone wears shoes. Unless you are working with a group from Harley Davidson, the question, "Do you like to ride a motorcycle?" is not likely to result in everyone checking the cup. These are the types of questions you want them to write. The questions should be at the category level and not too specific. For example, "Do you know Tom Cruise?" is too specific. You may ask however, "Do you know a celebrity?"

Keep in mind, you will want to make sure each cup has the same number of questions. If you have a few small groups of six people and the rest of the groups only have five people, you will ask the groups with five to include an additional question that is true for someone in their group.

Cup Networking Guidelines

When all the groups have written out their questions follow these steps:

- Have each small group give itself a name and write it on the bottom of their cup.

- Instruct each small group to pass their cup to the group on their right - each small group will have another group's cup after switching.

- Start a one minute timer (or start the stopwatch - going to one minute).

- Someone in each small group will read aloud the questions on the cup to his/her groupmates. The reader will make a check mark by the question for each person in the group that can answer the question as true for them - if a question is true for three people in the group, make three check marks. Go on to the next question.

- After one minute ask for all writing to stop.

- Have the small groups pass the cups to the right.

- After the pass the facilitator will start the one minute timer and checking begins.

- Continue passing cups, after every minute, until all small groups have had a chance to read all the other groups' cups and each group is finally in possession of their own cup.

- Each group is then tasked with counting the check marks on their cup. The group with the lowest number of check marks is crowned the most unique bunch pf people at that moment!

- Be sure to say that each team should never check off their own cup's questions (dah!). Have each small group give itself a name and write it on the bottom of their cup.

- Instruct each small group to pass their cup to the group on their right (counterclockwise) - each small group should have another group's cup.

- Instruct everyone to have one person from their group read the questions on the cup aloud to his/her groupmates - one at a time. The reader will make a check mark next to a question for each person in the group that answers Yes to that question. For example, if a question is true for three people in the group, The reader makes three check marks. Go on to the next question.

- Start a one minute timer. (You can be flexible with this time limit.)

- After one minute tell everyone to stop writing.

- Have the small groups again, pass the cups to their right.

- After the cups are passed, give the groups one minute to read the questions and add checkmarks to the cup.

- Continue passing cups, after every minute, until all small groups have had a chance to read all the other groups' cups and each group is once again in possession of their original cup.

- Each group is then tasked with counting the check marks on their cup. The group with the lowest number of check marks is crowned, The Most Unique Bunch of People! (At that moment.)

- Be sure to mention that each team should not check off their own cup's questions. (You know you've got to say it!)

Safety: Before you begin, remind everyone about mental and emotional safety issues. Ask them not to write questions that will embarrass or pressure anyone into any unnecessary confessions. Also, be sure to use "non-toxic" permanent markers for this one. (Do they still make the toxic markers?)

Facilitation: You may have to coach groups around including "fair" questions - ones that are not too specific. You could say something like, "If you are not sure about a question you could check it with me before writing it on your cup."

Adjust the time as needed depending on the size of the small groups. For example, if there are groups of eight people, you might want to have 90-second rotations between the passing of the cups.

We have found that breaking up the rules during the presentation leads to better clarity. For example, first share the rules about how to write the questions on the cups. Then allow them to do so before explaining how to play the game. Consider holding off sharing the rule about passing cups until the time is up for writing on the cups. In other words, share the rules when they become necessary.

Observations/Questions:
1. Discovering commonalities:
   A. Did anyone notice cups with similar questions?
   B. What does that tell you about your group?
   C. What is good about sharing commonalities with each other?
   D. What is good about having differences among each other?

2. Building relationships.
   A. How does sharing differences build relationships in your group?
   B. What drew you the most to your group?

C. How comfortable were you contributing a question to the cup?

D. Did it seem easier for some than others? Why do you think that is?

E. Did you ask for ideas? Are you comfortable asking for help?

3. Building trust:
   A. How did trust play into this activity?

   B. What question or questions did not get answered? Did you trust that others were being truthful, that someone actually did what was written?

   C. Did you think that any of the questions were too specific? How did you react to this?

4. Finding the fun:
   A. What, if anything, made this activity fun for you?

   B. Thinking back on the questions you encountered, which questions were the most fun for you?

   C. What question did you see/hear that you wanted to know more about?

   D. In general, what makes something fun for you - what are your "fun factors"?

E. When is the last time you had a lot of fun?
    What were you doing?

Variations :

- With groups smaller than 15 players, give a cup and a marker to each person. With five minutes on the clock have each player individually write six questions about themselves. During game play, rotate the cups to the right every 20 seconds. During each rotation players initial the questions on other players' cups that are true for them. After one complete rotation - each person reads over his/her own cup and counts initials. Find out who has the least number of questions initialed on their cup. Celebrate this person's (and everyone's) uniqueness.

- Have players write about themselves related to specific topics. For example, the facilitator will say, "Write questions related to hobbies you have or like." Or, "Write questions that are related to school" or, "work". As the group gets to know each other a little more, building more trust, you may choose to make the topics a little more personal. For example, "Write questions related to your family." Or, "Write questions related to any fears you have about the present or future." "Write questions about wishes and dreams."

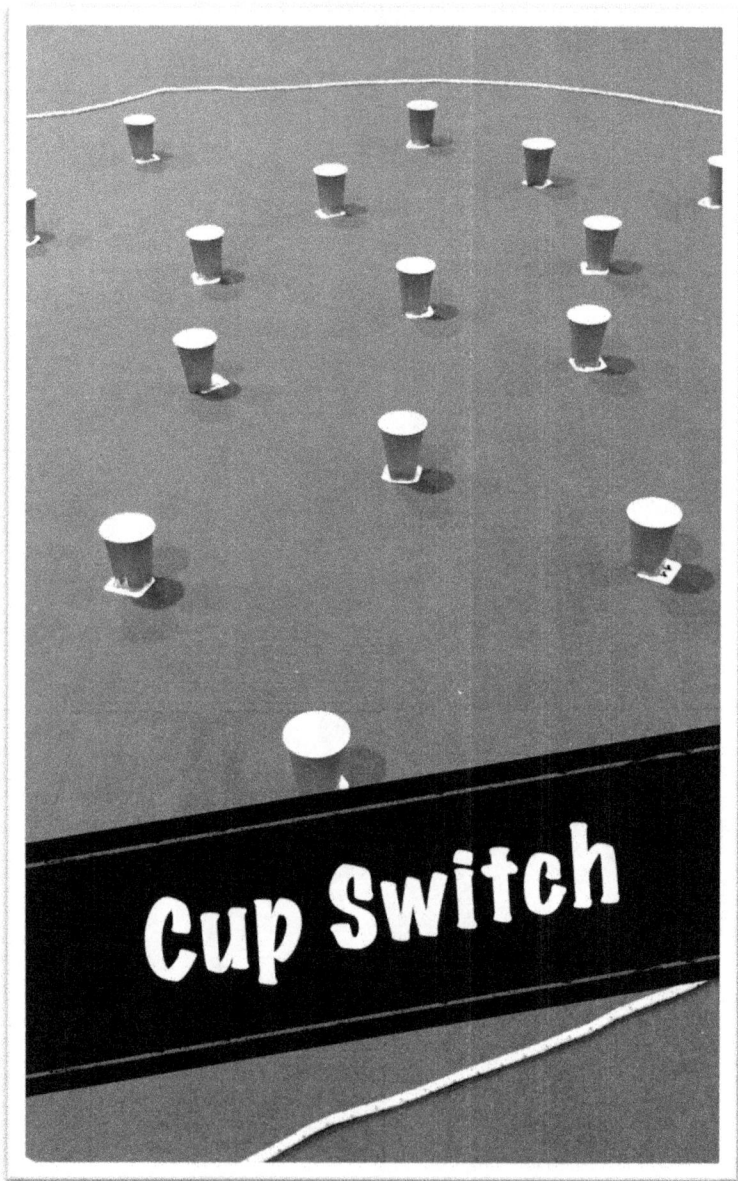

Cup Switch

CUP SWITCH

This activity first appeared at Chris' FUNdoing.com blog site as Tube Switch (November 24th, 2014). After substituting the equipment with cups we have a more complex version of the original idea.

Activity Objective: Match all the numbered cups with the numbered spots - only two cups can be moved at a time.

Facilitated Objective:

1. Planning, overall and in the moment.
2. Brainstorming and sharing ideas.
3. Leadership dynamics towards planning.
4. Understanding roles and responsibilities.
5. Communication behaviors.

Needs Per Group:

- 12 to 24 numbered or lettered cups

- 12 to 24 numbered spots or numbered index cards

- 1 50-foot activity rope

- 1 timing device

Cups are numbered or lettered on the bottom (see picture) - we like to make our numbers or letters as large as possible. A black or silver permanent marker, or a combination of both, leave good visible numbers or letters.

If you have the fancy numbered poly spots (like the ones in the picture above), they work great. Spots could also be numbered index cards or small paper plates, or even half sheets of paper. Be sure the numbers are smaller than the open end of the cups you are using - when you place a cup over a number (in the closed position) you do not want to see any part of the number on the spot.

Numbers: Four to 16 players. Multiple groups can play this one at the same time. Provide the same window of time for all groups (e.g., 20 minutes) to record their best time. If you have a larger group (12 to 16), consider splitting them up into smaller groups of equal numbers (or maybe not equal numbers depending on your objectives).

Time: 20 to 30 minutes.

Procedure: (For this description, imagine we are working with one group of 12 players using 20 numbered cups and 20 numbered poly spots - like the picture below.) Lay out your rope in a large circle (or other geometric shape) formation. Randomly set down your numbered spots (numbers up) so they are spaced out within the circle. Place a numbered cup, in the closed position, over each of the spots. Be sure the number on the bottom of the cup does not match the number on the spot.

When all the numbers on the spots are covered with cups bring your group over to the activity area and have them stand around the outside of the rope circle. Here is what we (generally) tell our groups.

Working together, your objective is to cover each

numbered spot, there is one under each cup, with its matching numbered cup as quickly and safely as possible. If any of the following parameters are violated the attempt in progress stops and time is set

to zero - another attempt can be made once the cups are reset.

If you are providing only verbal directions to the group, share the Cup Switch Guidelines below. If you want to forego giving all the directions verbally, print the Guidelines below and give them to your group. After you share the overall objective with them they can read the rest of the guidelines and then answer their own questions (with a little help from you if needed).

As always, feel free to adjust what you need to make the activity fit within your objectives.

Cup Switch Guidelines

- A cup may only be picked up by a person inside the cup area.
- When the first person steps into the cup area, the time will start.
- No more than two people can step inside the cup area at any time.

- Each person in the cup area is allowed to pick up and set down ONE cup - the cup you pick up is the cup you set down.

- Picking up a cup is the ONLY way the number on a spot can be revealed.

- The numbered spots must stay in their original location (i.e., no moving the numbers).

- Cups must be placed back down on a numbered spot, completely covering the number on the spot.

- After placing a cup, the person must exit the cup area - both feet stepping completely outside of the cup area.

- When each cup is covering its matching number someone in your group must tell the timer, "We're Done!" At this point the time stops.

- Before the official time is given, all matches will be verified.

To verify the matches, we ask all the players to step inside the cup area and slide the cups to the side of the numbered spots and then step out of the area. After a quick scan we can share the overall time or, if there is a mismatch, call the attempt "invalid".

When we have the time, and the group is willing and able, we ask them if they could do better (e.g., faster time, better process, whatever they want to improve upon). If so, ask the group to move off to the side away from the cup area (the objective here is to prevent participants from seeing the new setup) in order to plan for their next attempt. When the group is off planning, reset the cup area.

We have found (so far) the fastest process is to quickly collect all the cups into one stack. Then, we move about a third of the numbered spots around after which we place a cup over each numbered spot - be sure the cup number does not match the spot number. When the cup area is reset we invite the group back over to stand outside the geometric shape.

If the motivation is there, three or four rounds allows for opportunities to improve.

Safety: We have yet to see any major safety issues with this one. The one thing we do tell the group is to be careful when exiting the cup area. If someone is moving out quickly there is a chance of colliding with another person.

Facilitation: More often than not, after we present the directions to the activity, we hand someone in the group a copy of the Cup Switch Guidelines so they can refer to them when they have questions.

As for the "timer" - the person who will be timing each Cup Switch attempt – you can volunteer your services to be the timer or have someone in the group be the timer. Decide what will be the most appropriate for the group in relation to their program objectives.

As the facilitator you will also need to make the choice to be the referee or allow the group to call their own parameter violations - whatever fits the best with the group's objectives. As noted, any Guideline violations result in a restart.

Depending on the group and who is calling the violations, there could be several resets of the cup area. So, be sure to get a good night's rest and eat a healthy breakfast before the program.

Observations/Questions:
1. Planning, overall and in the moment:
    A. What were some of the initial reactions to the activity after you heard the rules?

B. How did these reactions contribute to the choices you made going into the activity?

2. Brainstorming and sharing ideas:
   A. How many of you had an idea about how to proceed with the challenge? Let's see a show of hands.
   B. How many of you had the opportunity to share your idea?
   C. How many of you did not have/take the chance to share your idea?
   D. What process could this group develop to make sure everyone has the opportunity to share their thoughts and ideas about something you are going to do together?

3. Leadership dynamics towards planning:
   A. What did the planning look and sound like in the beginning?
   B. Did everyone understand the plan before you started the activity? How do you know?
   C. Did the plan change during the activity? If so, in what way(s)?

   D. Why do you think plans change over the course of a task?

E. Can anyone share an example of a plan changing at another point in your life, and why do you think it changed?

4. Understanding roles and responsibilities: What roles and responsibilities did you discover to be necessary to your success?

   A. What role did you play during the activity? Was it assigned to you or did you choose the role? What is your preferred choice - someone choosing for you, or choosing the role you want to take?

   B. Did your role change during the activity? If so, why did it change?

5. Communication behaviors:

   A. What did the communication sound like and look like during the activity?

   B. What was working well for you in the area of communication?

   C. What one thing could be better about the way you communicated with each other?

Variations:

- Change Guideline #7 - this is a more challenging version of Cup Switch. Require participants to place cups on the numbered spots open end down. It will now be more challenging to remember which spots are covered by the matching cup. Here's how we reword Guideline #7: "All cups must be placed back on the numbered spots open end down, completely covering the number on the spot".

- Place the numbered spots inside the rope circle so that even numbers are located on one side/half of the circle and odd numbers on the other half/side of the circle. We don't make the split obvious with a space down the middle dividing the two sides, but you could. In this way, the group has an opportunity to discover that evens and odds are grouped together narrowing down the search area when looking for a particular number.

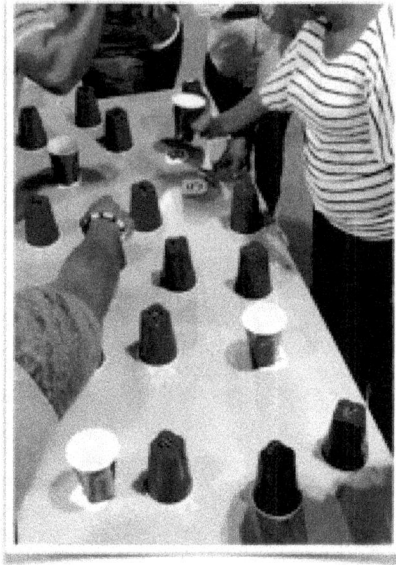

- Set up and play this one on a tabletop - one table for each group/team that is in play. This is a good set up for larger sized (more than 16 players). Each table set up can have six to 10 players around it. Tables, since they are higher off the floor, make the activity more accessible to different ability levels (and, age ranges).

- For a greater challenge, require participant pairs inside the cup area to pick up the cups at the same time (Thanks Ben V.) The Guidelines do not require this specific action, so if a pair inside the cup area chooses (figures out) the strategy where one cup is lifted first, revealing the number, the partner can then pick up the matching cup of the number revealed and move the match to cover the number. When both cups are required to be picked up at the same time, more memorization of numbers is required, making this variation a greater challenge.

82

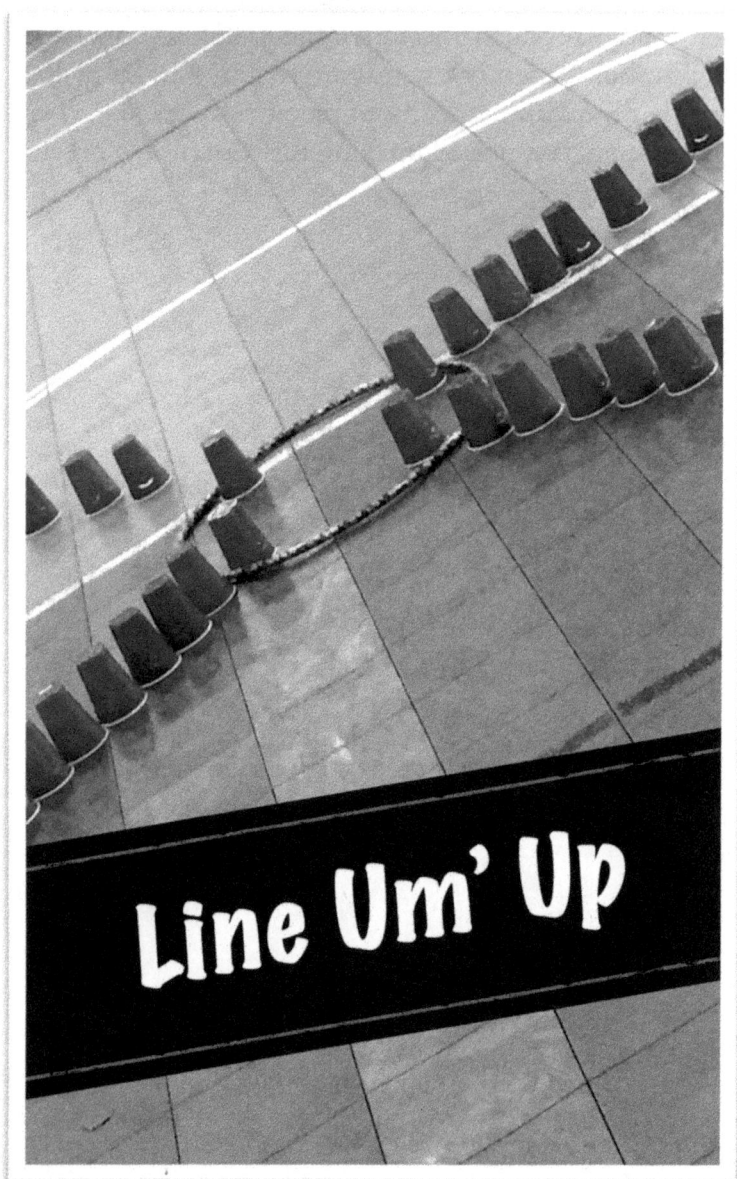

Line Um' Up

CupItUpTheBook.com - Chris Cavert & Barry W. Thompson

Line Um' Up

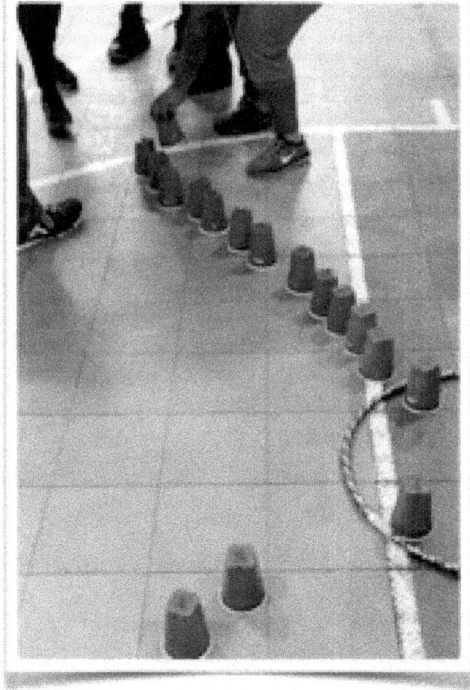

Line Em' Up evolved from two different activities,
When the Chips are Down from Sam Sikes and
Exchanging Knots from Mike Spiller. This adventure
involves the fast-paced line up from Sikes blended
with the collaborative opportunities from Spiller.

Activity Objective: As a group, line up all the cup
sets available in sequential order as quickly as possible.

Facilitated Objective:

1. Preparation and planning.
2. Recognizing and delegating roles and responsibilities.
3. Goal setting, collaboration and sharing information.
4. Competition.

Needs:

- 1 set of 26 numbered or lettered cups for each group in play

- 1 hula-hoop or webbing circle for each group in play

- 1 hula-hoop or webbing circle for the "Center Hoop/Ring"

- 1 timing device

If you are playing on a carpeted or tiled area you could also use masking tape to mark out cup and center areas (see Variations below).

Numbers: 12 to 30 players divided into three to six equal numbered groups.

Time: 25 to 35 minutes.

Procedure: (For this description imagine we're using hula-hoops with four teams of five players each. Set the hula-hoops on the ground/floor like the five pips on a die [If you didn't know, those little dots found on dice are called pips - who knew they had a name?!] - one hoop for the "center area" and one hoop at each of the corners (see picture above). Corner hoops are called the "cup-areas".

You'll want a minimum of 10 feet between the center area hoop and the four cup area hoops. If you want to add a bit more cardiovascular exercise to the activity, put the cup area hoops farther away from the center area hoop. (Webbing circles can be set up in the same configuration. If you use masking tape, simply tape out squares in the required configuration.)

Cup Preparation: Using your favorite brand of permanent marker write/draw numbers or letters on the bottom of a set of 26 cups - either 1 to 26, or A to Z (you'll need one set of numbered/lettered cups for each group/team in play).

If you want the option to present the Mix It Up variation (summarized below in Variations), you'll want each cup set of numbers or letters to look different from any other set (the picture shows some possible options on how to write/draw on the bottom of the cups).

For this example, we're using four sets of numbered and lettered cups - two sets of numbered cups and two set of lettered cups. One single set of nested cups is placed, one end up, in each one of the four cup areas, as shown in the picture above (no cups in the center area).

Before setting a stack down, the cups are shuffled within the stack so the numbers and letters start are in an un-sequential order. (This is not required, it just adds a bit more mystery to the first round. If players ask us if the cups are in order we answer them truthfully - we consider this "information gathering" during problem solving, and asking for help can be a productive behavior to acquire.)

The group of 20 (in our example) is divided into four small groups of five players each. A small group is assigned to each one of the cup areas. Before providing any of the directions for the challenge (telling them the directions or handing them a printed copy - found below), let the groups know they are all on the same clock - when all groups are finished, the time will stop. The challenge is to get the best (lowest) time possible for placing down all sets of cups, numbers and letters up (open ends down), in sequential order. All directions below must be followed for an official time to be recorded. And, a five-second penalty will be added to the overall time for each foul incurred.

On the following page are the main directions for Line Em Up. You can choose to read them to the group and/or give them a copy so they can read for themselves.

Directions for Line Em Up

- All cups must stay inside the cup areas, open end up, until time starts - looking at the numbers or letters on the bottom of any cup is prohibited until timing starts.

- Your facilitator will inform you of the game fouls, and the consequences for each, before the time starts.

- Cups can be arranged within each group's cup area in any way before timing starts - again, looking at any numbers or letters before time starts is prohibited.

- When each group is ready, timing will start.

- After the timing starts the cups can be turned over - players can look at the numbers or letters on the cups.

- Each player is responsible for placing at least one cup, number or letter up, within proper sequential order - 1 to 26 or A to Z.

- The first cup in each set, number "1" or letter "A", must be set down first, number or letter up, inside the center area.

- All remaining cups must be placed down one at a time in sequential order, independently of one another (not nested together), number or letter up, outside the cup areas.

- When ALL cups in play have been set down in sequential order (outside of the cup areas) the timing stops.

Fouls:
- The first cup ("1" or "A") is not in the center hoop after timing stops.

- A cup is set down out of sequence (e.g., "M" set down before "G").

- Someone does not set down at least one cup from his/her group's set of cups.

Consequence for a Foul:
For each foul committed five seconds is added to the overall time after an attempt.

Provide planning time before each attempt. (At least three timed attempts will be provided - see more below). Tell the groups to let you know when they are ready for the time to start. We tend to allow as much time as needed for planning. (It's a good discussion point at the end - "wait" management.) Tell your groups the time will stop when all the cups have been set down in sequential order.

After the first attempt add one more dynamic to the activity. Ask each team to collect their cups and arrange them, open end up, in any way they want, "that will lead them to greater success" inside of their cup area. When all the teams are satisfied with their arrangement, tell them this: "For the next 60 seconds no one is allowed to touch any cups." Then ask each team to.......(wait for it)........move clockwise to the next cup area. Now, they have one minute (or more if needed?) before the next timed attempt will start - no touching cups. (The hope is that teams will share how they arranged their cups for success!).

Each attempt from this point on will follow the same process. We've found that groups stay engaged through three or four attempts depending on their motivation to succeed - especially if they realize they can share their "cup-arrangement" information with the group that inherits their cup area or, they might even ask the group moving to their cups how they would like them set up.

Safety: So far we have not run into any safety issues related to Line Em' Up. There is some chaotic movement during the cup line-ups, but since there is no great distance between the cup-hoops and the center hoop body acceleration is kept to a minimum. In any case, we do make our participants aware of the possible collision factor.

Facilitation: The gem in this activity for us is the possibility of collaborative information sharing. The very first beta attempt (true story!) of Line Um' Up proved to be a very powerful lesson for the group. When each small team of adult youth group volunteers heard they were switching hoops after arranging their cups "just right," one team knocked over most of their cups and another team quickly put all their cups in a single nested stack (yes, we did tell them they were all on the same clock - twice). Not one team shared the arrangement they left behind with the team that followed them. We were hoping by the third (and final) round it would be different, but it wasn't. Since they expected to switch hoops the teams made no effort to arrange their cups in any way before they rotated. The discussion led to some fruitful considerations for this group as they moved forward in their volunteer work.

When considering the number of players in each small group, a smaller group size will require more work from each player but more verbal interaction. In a larger group, the work and verbal communication is more dispersed.

Another facilitation consideration we want to share is the role of timer. So far we have been doing the timing for the group - for reasons of accountability maybe?

Assigning this responsibility to (someone in) the group is another option. Especially if you choose to provide the Directions sheet. As we know, the more they are responsible for the process the more they can pull from the experience.

94

Observations/Questions:

1. Preparation and planning:
    A. After understanding the objective, what type of planning took place?
    B. What did you notice about working on the plan in small teams?
    C. What could have been different about the planning process?
    D. After making a plan, did you stick with it? Why or Why Not?
    E. What ideas were shared about preparing the cups?
    F. If you had an idea about preparing the cups did you have/take the opportunity to share it during any of the rounds? Why or Why Not?

2. Recognizing and delegating roles and responsibilities:
    A. What roles did you notice being played out during the activity?
    B. What role did you play? Were you assigned this role, did you ask for this role, or did you "take" this role?
    C. Did your role change at any time during the activity? Why or Why Not?

D. Was there a role that was not taken by anyone during the activity that might have led you to more success? If so, share you're thinking about what was missing.

3. Goal setting, collaboration and sharing information:
   A. How would you describe collaboration?
   B. Describe a time in your life when you were in a collaborative environment - what behaviors did you notice?
   C. Describe a time in your life when you were in an environment that was not collaborative - what behaviors did you notice?
   D. Describe any points during the activity when you were being collaborative?
   E. Were there other opportunities to be collaborative during the activity that were not taken? If so, explain what you observed.
   F. How might these collaborative opportunities have helped?
   G. Describe what you remember about any of the collaborative opportunities that took place - or could have taken place.
   H. What is your overall opinion at this time about goal setting?

I. What is the difference between a process oriented goal and a product oriented goal?

J. What goal(s) did you set during the activity?

K. Share your opinion about how goal setting helped or did not help during the activity?

L. Describe other situations you might find yourself in where goal setting would help you accomplish something?

4. Competition:

A. Do you think competition played any part in the activity?

B. Describe any of the competitive behaviors you noticed during the activity?

C. What influence did these behaviors have on the activity?

D. What competitive behaviors do you believe are productive and which ones are unproductive? Why do you think so?

Variations:

- With the process described above, do not rotate before the third round. Have each group stay at the cup area they ended with after the previous round - but don't tell them they are not rotating. Simply start the next round after the groups have had an opportunity to arrange their cup areas.

- Mix It Up: Each small group has a set of cups that are made up of cups from all the sets in the activity (be sure each set of numbers and letters look different). Each group will need to place down the same set of numbers or letters, so when the cups are turned over, the first step will most likely be getting like sets of cups together in some way. Then, cups can be placed down in sequential order. Or, the cups you get are the cups you place! (I know, crazy, right!)

- Set up the activity so the cup areas are in a linear configuration. This will then require the groups to decide where the first cup will be placed. Maybe you even require the initial cups to be touching each other.

- Remember, if you don't have hula-hoops use masking tape squares on the floor. You could also give each group a table to work on if you have them and the room to set them up - the top of the table is where the cups start from. Then, they are set down in sequence on the floor/ground.

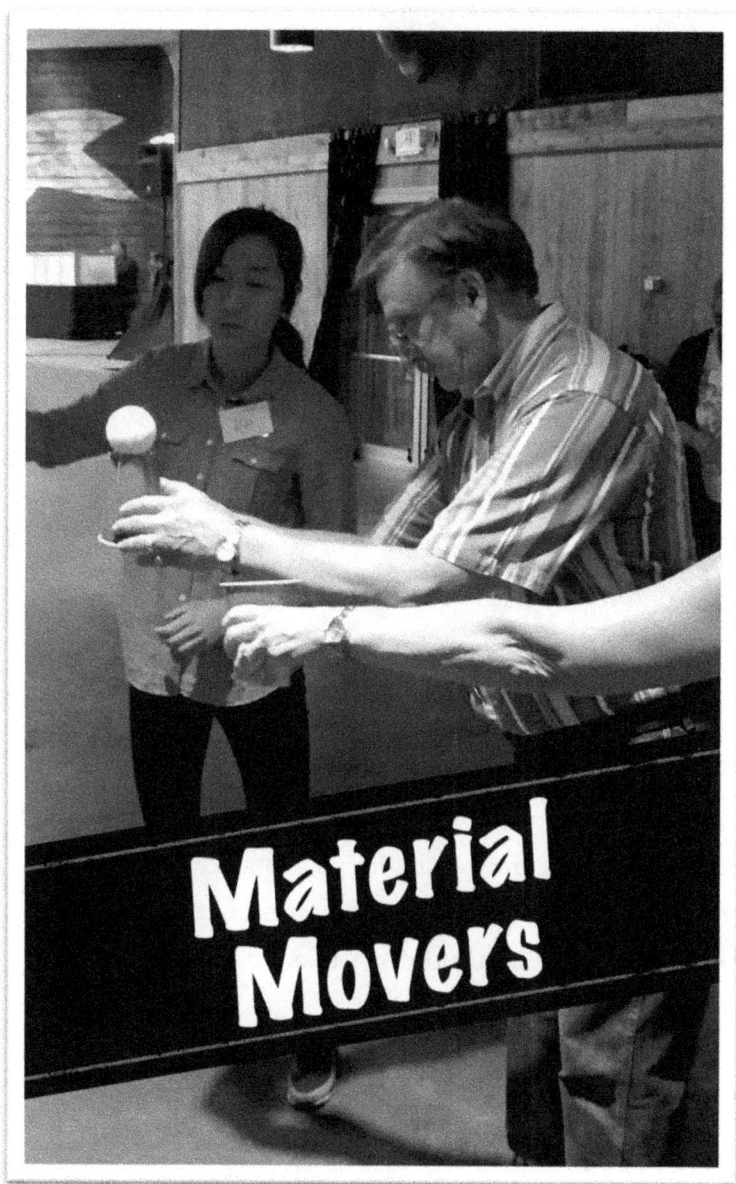

Material
Movers

Material Movers

We spun this one out of the activity Pipeline (credited to Lenny Diamond and popularized by Karl Rohnke, found in Karl's current, FUNN 'N' GAMES book). Using cups gives us a different challenge.

Activity Objective: Using cups - in a particular way - the group is challenged to move the material provided from one point to another with as little "loss" as possible.

Facilitated Objective:
1. Planning.
2. Foresight - anticipating challenges ahead.
3. Goal setting.

4. Resource management.
5. Linear communication - issues and solutions, cooperation and collaboration.
6. Working through mishaps and failure.

Needs:

*   1 cup for every participant in the group.

*   2 containers (buckets, bins or hula-hoops) for each small group (of four to eight participants) in play

*   5 game spots for each small group in play

*   100 tennis balls (or something similar) shared between all groups - these are the "materials" that will be moved (see below for other options).

Not everyone has 100 tennis balls on hand (but, if you do, there are lots of activities using tennis balls!). Materials could be a mixture of larger wooden blocks, other tossables about the same size as a tennis ball (small enough to fit in or on a cup), ping-pong balls & golf balls (these two material sources are a little small, but can work), PVC fittings or small PVC tube pieces, noodle poppers (a small 1.5 inch noodle slice cut in half), wadded up recycled paper held together with masking tape, or…you get the idea. You don't want to go too small (e.g., Legos or marbles) because you can move a lot of these items at one time which would make the activity a little too easy.

Numbers: This one works well with eight to 32 players. If you need to divide your large group into a number of smaller groups, make sure there are no more than eight people in a group.

Time: 20 to 30 minutes depending on the number of attempts provided.

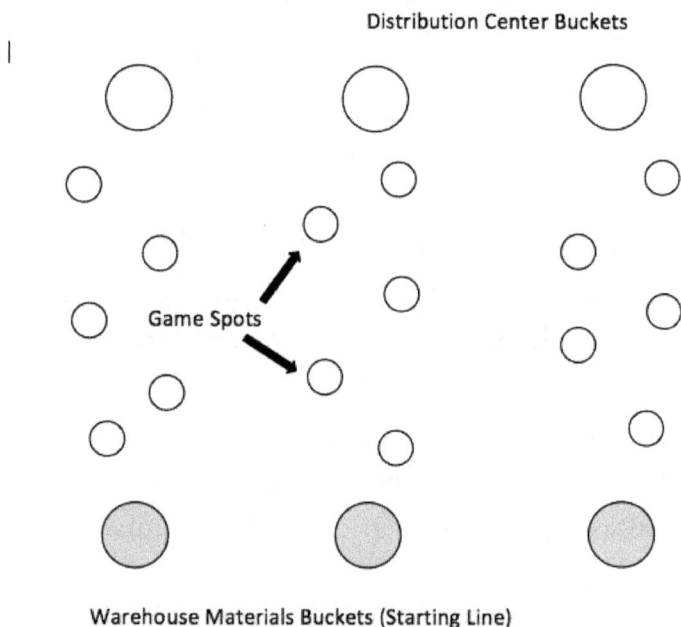

Distribution Center Buckets

Game Spots

Warehouse Materials Buckets (Starting Line)

Procedure: First construct your transit area as shown below. Set out one material bucket (bin or hula-hoop) for each group. When there is more than one group, space out the buckets along a straight line at least six feet apart from each other (see diagram above). The material bucket(s) will be the Warehouse(s) (WH) for the materials you will be asking your group to move. The WH bucket(s) will also be the starting line for the activity. The tennis balls (or other materials), will be equally distributed (inside) the bucket(s).

NOTE: If playing with only one small group, you might need two buckets to fit all of the material - just place the buckets right next to each other.

Next set one Distribution Center (DC) bucket down at the other end of the transit area - one across from each WH. How far apart? Let's say you are going to form groups of eight. Walk off about 10 feet of space for each person in the small group. So, for eight-player groups set down a DC bucket at least 80 feet from each WH bucket.

The diagram above is a set up for about 24 players - notice the DC buckets are about 80 feet from the WH buckets.

NOTE: If we are planning to allow for multiple attempts, we like to use buckets (instead of hula hoops). Why? After an attempt, it's easy to simply move the DC bucket(s) full of materials to the starting line of the transit area, making it/them the new WH bucket(s). If you only plan for one attempt placing all the materials in a hula-hoop makes for a good visual.

Once the WH and DC buckets are set, evenly distribute the 100 tennis balls between the WH buckets (if you only have one WH, all the tennis balls go in just the one - if they fit. Again, use two if needed). Put a nested stack of cups inside each WH bucket (make sure there is one cup available for each player).

Optional: If you want to add a bit more complexity to the activity, place five game spots in the transit area. Set them in a bit of a zig-zag pattern between each pair of buckets along the transit path (see diagram above). Use the spots as described in the directions below.

After your set up is complete, divide your overall group into smaller groups of four to eight players. Have each small group stand near the WH bucket(s) of tennis balls before providing the directions.

Okay! Let's Get Started

Explain the overall objective of the activity: Move the 100 tennis balls provided from the Warehouse bucket(s) to the Distribution Center bucket(s) with as little loss as possible. "Loss" is defined as tennis balls that end up on the floor/ground. (Using 100 tennis balls makes for easy "percentage" math and for grading the activity when working with school-aged participants.)

Then ask the "whole" group (all small groups together) to decide what their acceptable losses will be (i.e., the maximum number of tennis balls that end up on the floor/ground). You can present this goal setting process before or after you give the directions. We like to do this before since groups often make assumptions about what they will be doing after seeing the equipment.

Directions:

- Each player can use one, and only one, cup during the process of moving the provided material (e.g., tennis balls).

- You may not relinquish (give away) your cup during the activity.

- Cups can move materials in two different ways - the "Pour" and the "Transfer". For the pour, the cup starts in the open position. One, or more, of the materials are inside the cup and are then poured into or onto another cup. For the transfer, a cup starts in the closed position. Material is on the bottom of the cup and then "transferred" onto or into another cup. (Notice the two cup positions in the picture above.)

- After you use one of the moving techniques with your cup (the pour or the transfer), you must move material using your cup the other way.

- Once your cup has moved into a new position (open or closed) it may not be turned in any way until there is material in or on the cup.

- If any material is dropped onto the floor/ground during a pour or transfer, you must still complete the cup rotation. The cup must then be used to move material from its new position.

- When there is material in or on your cup you may not move your feet. You may move any other part of your body.

- Material may only be touched by someone's hand (or any other body part) when being taken out of the WH bucket(s) to be placed in or on a cup.

- Material may only touch cups when in the transit area between the WH bucket(s) and the DC bucket(s). If the material touches anything other than the cups while in transit (e.g., someone's finger) it must be dropped to the floor/ground.

- Material that is dropped or falls to the floor/ground is left where it lands. The facilitator may move material out of the way if it presents a safety issue. Note: Moving it may also prevent the material (e.g., ping-pong balls) from being destroyed.

- If you choose to stand on one of the spots found in the transit area you are free to use your cup in either of the two ways (pour or transfer). However, as soon as you stand on a spot (one foot or two) your eyes must be closed. When you leave a spot, your cup must go to the closed position, ready to transfer material. NOTE: Spots may not be moved.

- When there are no more materials left in the WH buckets to move, the activity is over. You will then have the opportunity to assess your losses and determine what happens next.

Safety: The only potential hazard we have seen so far, and have prepared groups to look out for, is the ankle rolling potential of stepping on material (e.g., tennis balls) on the floor/ground. In most cases we simply remind the players of the hazards laying around. We will make a conscious effort to move material away from the players with their eyes closed due to the heightened risk. We also make sure players refrain from throwing material if we hear or see a plan taking shape of that nature.

Facilitation: There are a few subtleties that you may want to consider when programming Material Movers. The amount of material you use and the distance between buckets (start to finish) will have a direct correlation to the length of time needed for the activity. More stuff and more distance = more time needed. We like the "100" pieces of material and the 10 feet of space for each person in a small group. If you provide more or less material, and more or less distance to travel, your goal language might change. (And, you'll also have to do the percentage math for the material if you use more or less than 100 of something.)

The type of materials you use can change the activity as well. If you use only round objects (e.g., tennis balls, ping-pong balls, etc.) the likelihood of drops using transfers increases without a plan to prevent potential drops. If flat-sided material is provided (e.g., large building blocks, PVC fittings, etc.) transfers are a little easier.

So far, we have only seen small groups work together linearly to move materials. We have yet to (but would like to) see players break ranks to help other sub-groups. Players tend to stay with the role of "movers" when "protectors" of material (especially during a transfer) would help prevent loss. However, we will assume when groups choose a more challenging material "loss" goal (or are "encouraged" to do so), this will increase the potential for creating other roles and helping behaviors.

What we have found to be the most interesting part of Material Movers is how the players adapt their process after a drop occurs. If a small group chooses to form one line (the plan we've seen the most), and pass along materials down this line, a drop will cause some dissonance. In most cases drops happen during the transfers. If this happens players in line will have cups held in both positions - open and closed. This situation forces them to change some of, or all of, their original plan, possibly utilizing the spots available, collaborating, or even dumping materials back into the WH (we didn't say they couldn't), so they can get back on track. When the small groups (we hope) realize they can collaborate with each other to be more successful, drops can cause cross pollination of cup positions to lead them to success. The unpredictable opportunities make for some good discussions.

Finally, you will want to decide how many attempts to give your group. We like to provide at least two attempts in order to allow for an opportunity to improve. If you have time to allow a third attempt, even better.

Observations/Questions:
1. Planning:
   A. What did your planning look like and sound like before you started the activity?
   B. Did everyone have the opportunity to share her or his voice during the planning stage?
   C. What are some aspects of your planning sessions that you believe could have been better?

2. Foresight - anticipating challenges ahead:
   A. What do you know about the idea of foresight?
   B. What challenges were you able to foresee in the activity?
   C. What helped you to foresee these events?
   D. What challenges were you unable to foresee?
   E. What prevented you from anticipating these events?
   F. Describe how you handled the unforeseen

   events?

3. Goal setting:
   A. What roles and responsibilities did you determine to be necessary before you began the activity?
   B. What helped you to recognize the roles and responsibilities needed?
   C. What new roles and responsibilities needed to be filled during the activity - after you got started?
   D. Did anyone see a role that needed to be filled? If so, what did you do about it?
   E. Looking back over your process, would you eliminate and/or add any roles and responsibilities that might help you reach a higher level of success (i.e., less loss)?
   F. What was your overall "loss" goal for the activity? How did you come up with this percentage/number?
   G. Did everyone agree with the goal? How do you know?
   H. Did everyone have/take the opportunity to share their thoughts about the goal? How do you know? If not, what prevented you from sharing your opinion about the goal?

I. What behaviors from the group would allow you to feel more comfortable sharing your ideas and opinions in the future?

4. Resource management:
   A. How did you "label" your materials? Easy to use? Difficult to use? What did this depend upon?
   B. What challenges did you encounter?
   C. How did you decide to manage the challenges?
   D. At this point, can you see other ways to manage the challenges you encountered?

5. Linear communication - issues and solutions, cooperation and collaboration:
   A. How would you define "linear" communication?
   B. What are some of the challenges you encountered with linear communication?
   C. What could you do in the future to work around linear communication challenges?
   D. How would you define cooperation?
   E. Was there cooperation going on during the activity?
   F. What did the cooperation look like? What did it sound like?
   G. What is collaboration?

H. Did any collaboration take place during the activity? What did it look like? What did it sound like?

I. What would you say (or know) about the difference between cooperation and collaboration? How can you use this information?

6. Working through mishaps and failure:
   A. Did you encounter any "failure" during the activity?
   B. What did you consider a failure before or during the process?
   C. How did you react or respond to the failure?
   D. Does failure motivate you or stop you?
   E. What are the ways we can view failure?
   F. How can we define failure?
   G. Is willing to share a story about how failure motivated you?

Variations:

- For a less complex scenario do not put spots down in the transit area.

- Set up the transit area in a big circle. Set down Warehouse buckets at 12, 4 and 8 o'clock and Distribution Center buckets at 6, 10 and 2 o'clock. See what happens when groups need to cross each other's paths.

- As noted above, use a variety of round and flat materials to vary the complexity.

- Use different sized cups: 18 and 12-ounce cups and maybe even some of those really small single-use paper cups. What about cone-shaped cups? Transfers could be tricky, but doable. Using different sized cups changes the process to allow more diverse perspectives and resource management systems. What can/will you do with the resources you have?

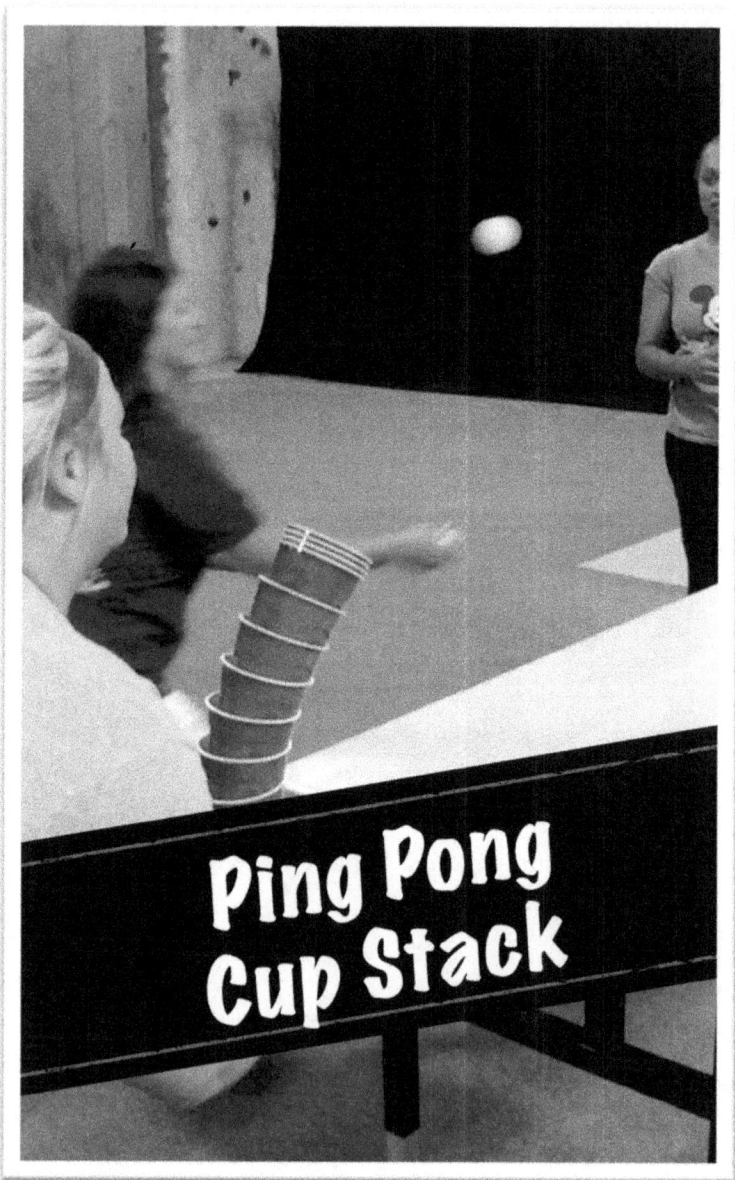

Ping Pong Cup Stack

Ping Pong Cup Stack

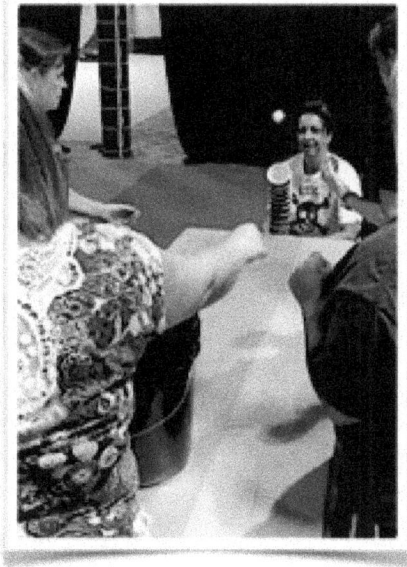

This activity was inspired by Tilt a Cup from the NBC hit show Minute To Win It. We added more people to make it a team challenge.

Activity Objective: Be the first team to bounce a ping pong ball into each of the 12 cups provided - making each cup float above the one below.

Facilitated Objectives:
1. Understanding roles and responsibilities.
2. Persistance.
3. Adaptability.

4. Supporting and encouraging teammates.

Needs Per Group:
- 12 cups.
- 12 ping pong balls.
- 1 container (e.g., small bucket) to hold the ping pong balls.
- 1 elevated bouncing surface such as a wooden or metal table or a ground-level surface such as a tile or wooden floor.

Numbers: Plays well with 12 to 32 participants. You will be forming small groups of four to eight people.

Time: 10 to 20 minutes depending on the number of games you play.

Procedure: Each small team of four to eight players will gather around their bouncing surface. Imagine we are using elevated six-foot long tables, one for each team. Arrange the tables side-by-side. Place a nested stack of 12 cups in the open position at one end of each table and the bucket of ping pong balls at the opposite ends of the tables. The roles, that continuously change, in the activity include one catcher, one bouncer, and retrievers (all remaining players on the team). With each small team encircled around their table, the players at each end of the table (the catcher and bouncer) start the game. This is a race between all the teams in play to see who can be the first to bounce a ping pong ball into each of the 12 cups in their stack.

The catcher at one end of the table (not the participants at the sides of the table) will hold the nested stack of cups - open end up. When playing the role of catcher, players may only hold/touch the bottom cup of the stack. The stack of cups may not be touched by anyone else or supported by anything else once the ball contacts the bouncing surface.

The bouncer, at the other end of the table, will access the bucket of ping pong balls. He/she will bounce one ping pong ball at a time off of the bouncing surface (e.g., table) towards the catcher. The ball must bounce at least once before it can go into the cup stack - it can bounce more than once.

The cup holder will attempt to catch the bouncing ball in the top cup. (The ping pong ball may not be caught after a roll.) If the catcher misses the ping pong ball it is collected up by one of the retrievers standing around the sides of the table, and then put back into the ping pong ball bucket. The bouncer picks out another ping pong ball to bounce towards the catcher - he/she does not have to wait for the missed ping pong ball to be placed in the bucket before bouncing.

When a ping pong ball is bounced and makes it into the top cup, the cup at the bottom of the stack is removed and placed inside the top cup over the ping pong ball (as depicted in the graphic below). Then the stack of cups is passed to the right - to one of the retrievers. The entire team rotates to the left allowing the new catcher to be at the catching end of the table and a new bouncer to rotate into the bouncing end of the table (the "old" bouncer and catcher move into the retriever role). In other words, players are not allowed to rotate until the pair of bouncer and catcher get a ping pong ball into the top cup of the tower. This bounce, catch, cup move, and player rotation process continues until all 12 ping pong balls are caught - at which point the victors (except for the cup holder) jump up and celebrate with some extreme volume.

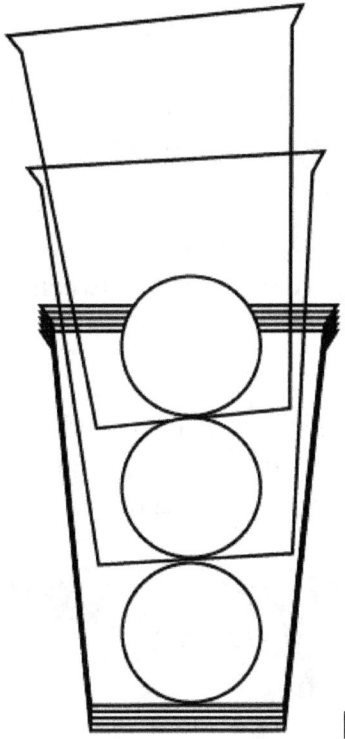

If the tower of "floating" cups, or any part of it, happens to crash to the ground, the players can put their tower back together in cup-ball order to where it was before the fall and then continue the bouncing catching process.

Safety: There will be a lot of chaotic movement around the playing area when the ping pong balls are missed. Keep reminding everyone to be careful when retrieving the strays.

Facilitation: Demonstrating how the cups are stacked helps with the visual understanding of the game. You can use this activity as an icebreaker or fun filler to get the group energized and moving. We like to use this activity as an active transition between icebreakers and team initiatives.

Be sure to have extra ping pong balls and cups available to trade out for any damage that occurs during the floating tower creation attempts.

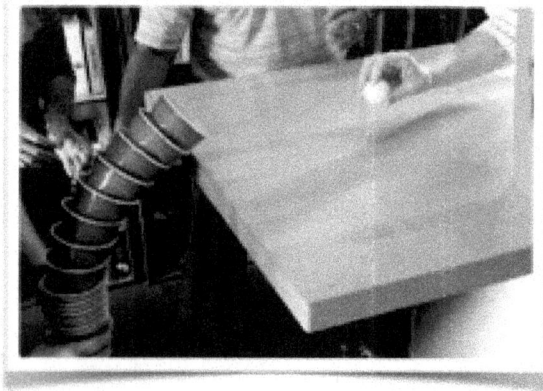

Observations/Questions:
1. Understanding roles and responsibilities:
    A. What were the responsibilities of each role?
    B. Which of the roles did you find most challenging?

C. Were there any other roles established during the activity and why?

D. Did the roles change at any time? How did they change?

E. How did you adapt to any role changes?

2. Persistence:
   A. How do you define persistence?
   B. During the activity, when did you need to be persistent?
   C. What is important about persistence?
   D. What motivates someone to be persistent?

3. Adaptability:
   A. Did you find it necessary to adapt during the activity?
   B. Explain the reasons why you found it necessary to adapt?
   C. Why is it important to adapt to certain situations?

4. Supporting and encouraging teammates:
   A. What did you notice about the language being used during the activity?
   B. What type of language was used when those "less skilled" took longer to catch the ball?

C. What about the "more skilled players" - what words were used when communicating with them?

D. How can the language we use affect the skills and behaviors of others?

Variations:

- Play a second game - rematch! But this time, instead of taking the bottom cup and moving it to the top of the stack after a ping pong ball catch, move the top cup (with the ping pong ball in it) to the bottom of the stack of cups. The "top-heavy" tower will be a little more challenging to operate for the second attempt.

- Allow the cup stack to be supported in other ways. For example, let the cup tower lean against the edge of the table or allow another player to help hold the tower. Do not give suggestions but allow for creative freedom.

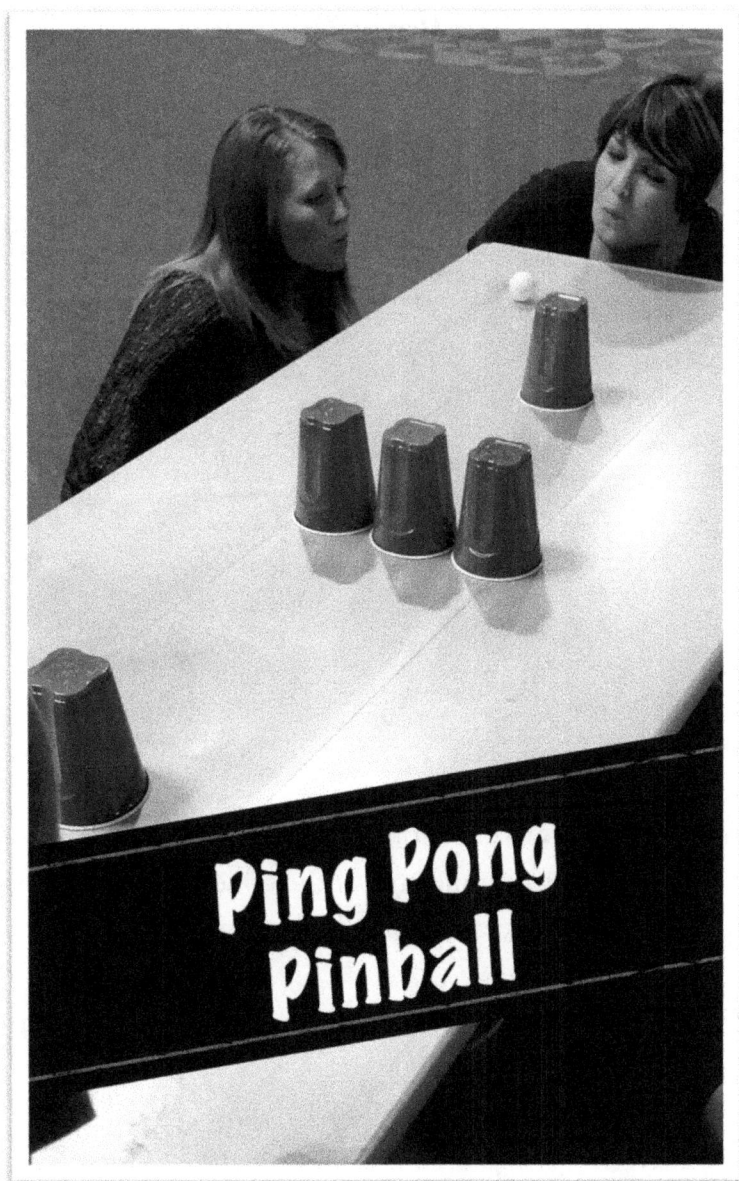

Ping Pong
Pinball

Ping Pong Pinball

This game started without cups - we called it Table Target. Adding cups has made it more like a team pinball game.

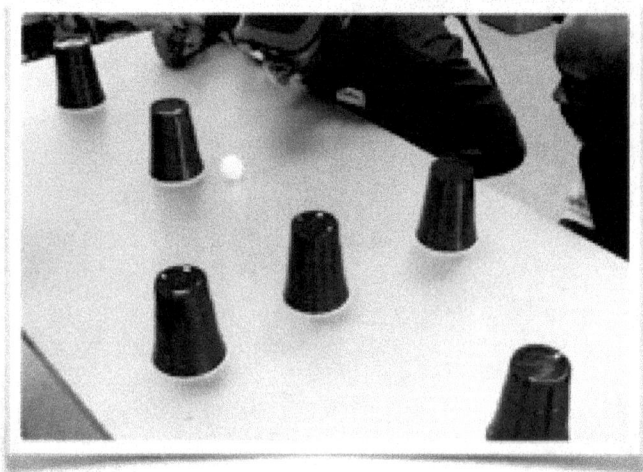

Activity Objective: Slalom a ping pong ball through a series of cups from one end of the table to the other as quickly as possible using only lung power.

Facilitated Objectives:
1. Sharing ideas.
2. Planning and practice.
3. Strategizing, failure and success.

Needs Per Group:

- 1 table

- 1 ping pong ball

- 7 cups (depending on the challenge level)

- 2 strips of 4-inch masking tape

- 1 timing device

- 1 piece of paper

- 1 pen or marker

Numbers: Four to eight players per table depending on the size of your tables. Any size group can play, divided into small groups, if you have enough of the equipment listed.

Time: 15 to 20 minutes depending how many rounds you play.

Procedure: Provide each small group with the supplies listed above. The goal for the activity is to have the ping pong ball slalom through a series of cups from one end of the table to the other as quickly as possible.

Using only the materials provided, each small group must plan out how the they are going to set down their cup slalom course on the table. Before setting the cups on the table they must first write/draw out a course plan on the piece of paper. Using all the cups is not required but they must use at least three.

This allows groups to create and set up the level of challenge they desire.

There must be a beginning (Point A) and an end (Point B) on each group's course. These points are identified with masking tape (see points A & B on the first diagram below). Tell the groups they will have 10 minutes to plan, practice and accomplish the activity. Groups can make as many timed attempts as they can within the 10 minutes. Once timed attempts begin, the cup slalom course may not be changed in any way, and no one can touch the cups. All timed attempts must start with the ping pong ball on the starting line tape (Point A).

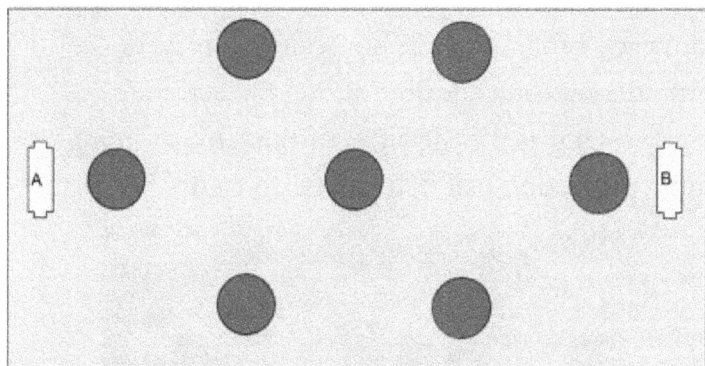

If a cup is touched during play, 30 seconds must be added to the group's overall time for that attempt. Groups must record (write down) their own times on their paper and turn it in to the facilitator when the 10 minutes is called.

If the ping pong ball falls off the table, that race attempt is over. When the ping pong ball crosses over the finish line tape (Point B), time can be stopped. During play, if a cup is moved by accident (lung power moves the cup), then it is up to the group to return it to its original placement before the next attempt is made.

Additional examples of cup slalom courses are provided below.

Safety: When there is more than one group playing, make sure you place the tables at least six feet apart from each other. You do not want the players bumping into one another during the action (e.g., while moving along the sides of the table or going after a ping pong ball that has fallen to the floor).

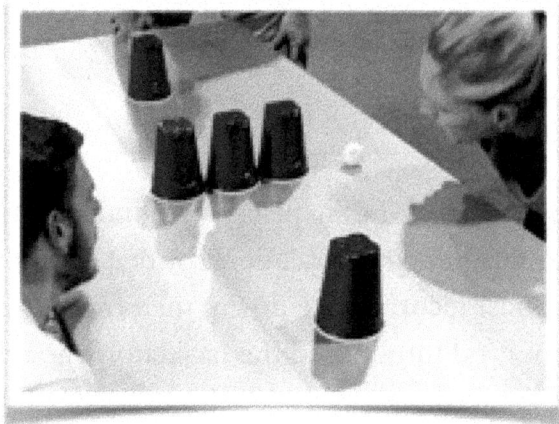

Facilitation: As the facilitator, you can either verbalize the directions or hand out a set of written rules included on their piece of paper (that you have created). Written rules can help you be more consistent when answering questions, since you don't have to remember what you said to the group.

Be sure to have extra paper available for the teams that need more creative working space and time.

Observations/Questions:

1. Sharing ideas:

    A. When you first got started, how did you share ideas about the task? What did this process sound like?

    B. Were all ideas shared and heard?

    C. If you had an idea that wasn't heard, what did you do about it?

    D. If you heard an idea from someone that wasn't heard by the rest of the group what did you do?

    E. What are some good ways to share ideas?

    F. How can we make sure everyone has the opportunity to share their ideas in the future?

2. Planning and practice:

    A. Describe what you remember about how you planned to put together your slalom course? For example, did you talk a lot about your course, did you just jump in and put something together to try out, or was it a little bit of both?

    B. What behaviors did you notice during the planning? For example, did anyone go off and plan by themselves or was there someone wanting to invite others in on the planning process? What does that say about your group?

C. Who was in charge of the planning session when you finally set up your course on the table? For example, was it just one person or a number of people?

D. In what way(s) did you contribute to the planning session?

E. What was good about the planning session?

F. Did the actual attempt turn out to be the same as the actual plan? If not, what was different about it?

3. Strategizing, failure and success:

A. What strategies did it take for you to control the ball as a team?

B. Were you able to develop your strategies before you started practicing or did you find that your strategies changed after some practice?

C. With each round did the strategy change and to what degree?

D. Once you started your race attempts for time, did you stick with the strategies you practiced or did they continue to change? Why do you think this happened for you?

E. Describe the failures you encountered during the races?

F. What did you do as a group to try to prevent

these failures in later races?

G. How did you react to the failures you encountered during practice?

H. How did you react to the failures you encountered during the timed races?

I. How do certain reactions to failure affect future experiences?

J. Did the number of practice attempts increase or decrease your success level? Why do you think this happens?

K. If this happened, did you notice different behaviors with regard to being conservative (less) in the number of cups at the beginning of the activity versus an "all cups in" mentality towards the end?

L. Which skills needed for this task were you most comfortable with?

M. Which skills needed for this task were you uncomfortable with?

N. How did your comfort level for each skill contribute to your success or failure during the activity?

Variations:

- One variation of the game is to purposefully hit all the cups before crossing the finish line. Seven rounds are played. Each round must be accomplished within a certain amount of time - you can decide the times for each round depending on the amount of challenge you want to present to your group. The first round only has one cup. If the ball falls off the table or touches the finish line tape before hitting all the cups on the table you have to start that round over. Each round add another cup to the table

- For a super challenge, the ping pong ball must completely circle around each cup on the table before it crosses the finish line - the ball can touch the cups.

- Use two ping pong balls (maybe different colors or markings) - start one on each end of the table. Each ping pong ball must accomplish the requirements and cross the tape on the opposite side of the table (Thanks Ben V.)

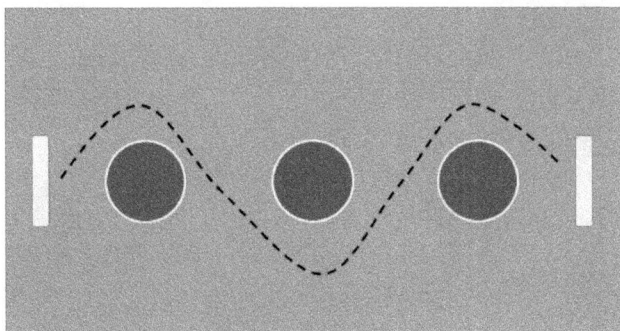

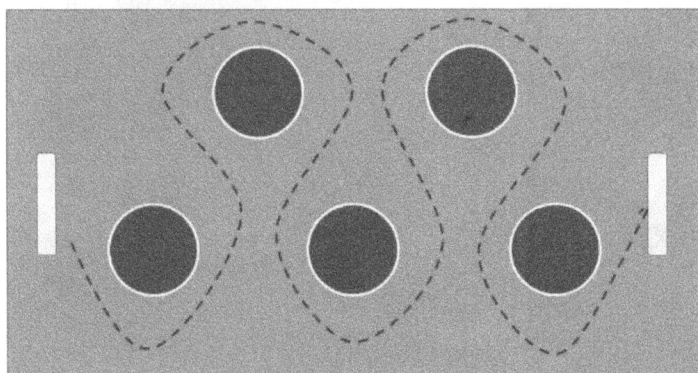

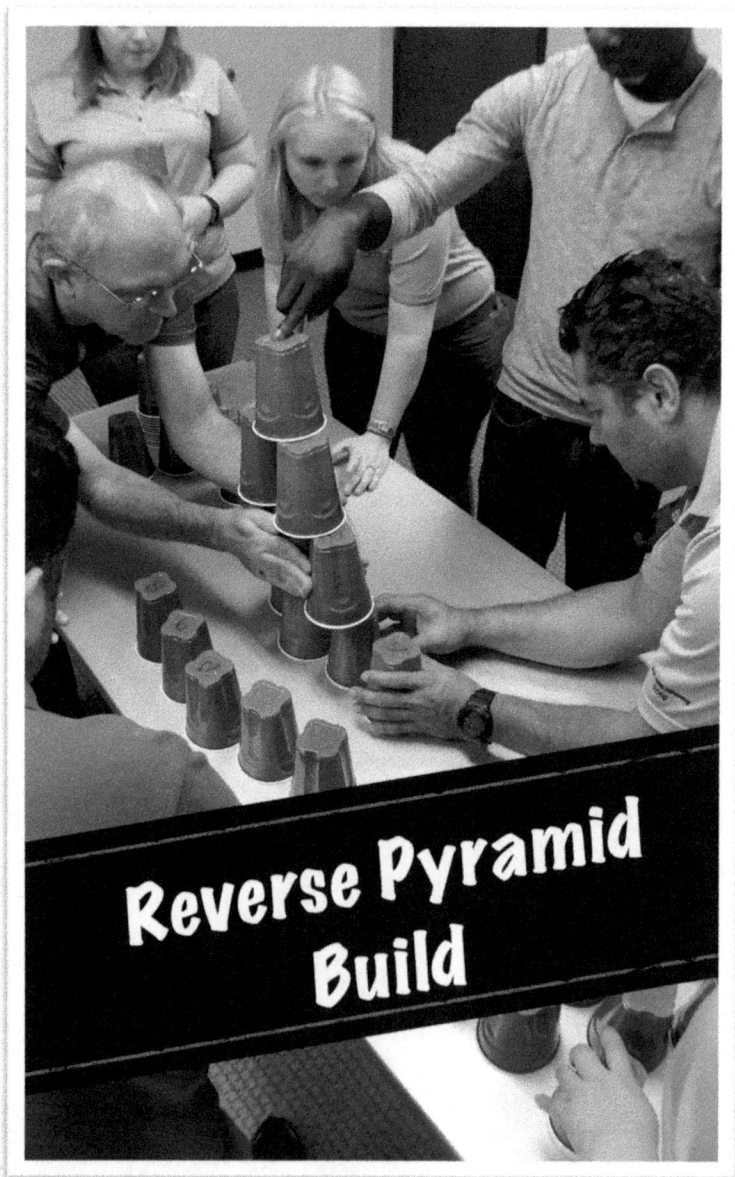

Reverse Pyramid Build

Reverse Pyramid Build

Activity Objective: Build the tallest cup pyramid starting with the top level of a single cup.

Facilitated Objective:
1. Small group interaction.
2. Communication behaviors.
3. Identifying, delegating, and taking on different roles and responsibilities.
4. Encountering and managing failure.
5. Perseverance.

6.   Consensus building.

Needs Per Group:

*   36 cups (It will be good to have extra cups available in case more building levels can be achieved.)

*   1 table for each small group - rectangle tables work out the best allowing a group to be closer to their pyramid structure. However, wooden platforms, flat-top benches, or picnic tables are other options.

NOTE: We have done builds Reverse Builds off of the floor (solid concrete or tile), but it's a bit more challenging to get enough bodies around the structure to support the lifts. Here's a thought: What about a 2x6-inch board about four feet long balanced across two chairs as a viable option for a building surface? Be creative in order to meet your needs.

Numbers: Create small groups of five to seven players. If you have enough cups and tables one facilitator can manage as many as 10 groups building at a time.

Time: 20 to 30 minutes

Procedure: Based on the dynamics of the Reverse Build, we consider this a small group activity (so far, anyway). Groups of five to seven players have worked well for us. If the situation arises where one group needs more hands they can ask players from another group to help. (This consideration might not work if the build is set up as a competitive activity. Notice, we did say "might not" work. We've seen competitors help each other.)

Give each group a nested stack of (36) cups and a designated building area. Here is generally what we say when we present the activity:

For each small group, your objective is to build the tallest pyramid using the cups provided. In our definition, a pyramid consists of stacked rows of cups (not a nested stack) in which each row will have one less cup than the row below it. For this build however, you are required to start from the top row of the pyramid - one cup. To begin, set this one cup down on your building surface. Then, anyone in your group can lift this first cup so that two cups can be placed under it, forming the second row of the pyramid. From this point forward you are only allowed to lift the bottom row of your pyramid structure - the row touching the table - to add the next row underneath.

All other cups in the pyramid can be touched or supported by any players index fingers (only) before, during and after a lift, but they may not be grabbed and/or lifted in any way. Again, only the bottom row of the pyramid can be lifted. If any part of your pyramid structure falls apart you must start your building process over from one cup. If you manage to use all the cups provided at the start of the build, more will be given to you. After I answer any questions you have about the directions, you will have 15 minutes of building time to see how high you can get your pyramid.

Most facilitators will answer questions without giving solutions to the challenge given. (However, if the group's objectives allow for help or "coaching", answer in the way that will work for them.) We often simply refer back to the rules provided. See Facilitation below for some typical inquiries.

This general presentation does not suggest any sort of competitive encounters. However, if you've been leading team building activities long enough, you know, in most cases, the competitive spirit does present itself. In the short life of this activity so far, we have yet to see groups help each other, but our hopes are still high. We typically run the build for about 15 minutes to see how well each group can perform. Success is fairly certain for the first three or four rows. After, four rows it's up to the creativity, focus and tenacity of the group. Cups will be falling. We keep encouraging attempts as long as there is time to build.

When our program objectives include competitive activities, we set it up a bit differently. We allow the small groups four to five minutes to practice and form a building plan. Then we give a 10-minute building window to achieve the tallest pyramid possible. They can use their 10 minutes in any way they like, as long as they stay around their building area (table) during the build. When the 10 minutes is up (i.e., when we say "Stop!") all the cups standing are worth a point value. How you score it will be up to you. We give one point for every cup that is touching another cup in a row above or below it. Or, simply count the number of rows - there are more ties in this scoring method.

As you might have determined already, the Reverse Build does not require a high level of energy, but a determined amount of focus. So, choose wisely when programming this one - what groups will benefit from this type of activity and where do you place it in your sequence?

142

Safety: At this time, no real safety issues have been observed. Bodies do tend to get pretty close to each other during the lift, so potentially some space issues could emerge.

Facilitation: During the Reverse Builds we have facilitated so far we have found it important to provide our expectations of the pyramid structure. When beta testing this activity a number of groups spent a lot of time trying to find loopholes in the rules and spent little time building. We wanted this activity to help us work on the facilitated objective of working through/with failures - since, in most cases, cup tumbling does occur during the process. When we started sharing our expectation of a pyramid more hands-on building ensued. The following is the sentence in the directions that specifies our expectations:

A pyramid is defined as each row (not a nested stack) of cups will have one less cup than the row below it.

During the cooperative version we move around the groups and continue to encourage working together and starting over after a collapse. We like to reiterate that the build is about "sticking to it", overcoming the collapses (great metaphor to come back to), and improving to the best of your ability. We also use this one in the hopes that groups will share strategies and maybe even resources (e.g., people) to help others be successful.

During the competitive version we have seen two different trends. Die hard builders (DHBs) and waiters (in the act of waiting - not waiting tables). DHBs are motivated by building the tallest pyramid, using all the time allotted - especially if they know the "world record" (to date eight rows - eight cups at the bottom level - is the highest for a group of seven players following the guidelines above (see Variations below for another presentation option and world record).

Waiters will build the highest pyramid in relation to other groups. If they see another group has five cups at their base the waiters will go to six cups. If a group gets six cups the waiters try for seven. If they find themselves in the lead with time left they will wait it out to see if they stay on top. Some will even be happy with a tie if little time remains. All good things to discuss once the activity is over.

One more thing we would like to share at this time. If you have the opportunity to build outside atop a solid flat surface, be mindful of the wind. It can be an asset or a detriment depending on your group's goals.

Observations/Questions:

1. Small group interaction:
    A. Rate, on a scale of one to five by holding up your fingers on one hand, how well your group worked together. Five is "the best group work ever" and a one is, "we need lots of improvement." If you didn't give your group a five, what would it take from the group to raise your rating one point?

B. What is your comfort level working with groups? Do you prefer to work in groups or on your own? Why do you think that is for you?

C. What is the most challenging thing for you to overcome when working with a group?

2. Communication behaviors:
   A. What did the communication sound like and look like during the activity?
   B. If you could change one thing about the way you communicated with each other during the activity what would it be?

3. Identifying, delegating, and taking on different roles and responsibilities:
   A. What roles and responsibilities did your process include?
   B. How did these roles and responsibilities get delegated?
   C. During your process did you find/discover the need for any additional roles and responsibilities?
   D. Did any of the roles and responsibilities change after you started your process? Why did this happen?

4. Encountering and managing failure:

A. What did you find yourself focusing on more - your successes or your failures?

B. What did you find yourselves doing after the cup collapses?

C. What choices do you have after a "failure"?

5. Perseverance:
    A. What does perseverance mean to you?
    B. At any point during the activity did you find yourself persevering?
    C. Which part(s) and why did you feel the need to persevere through the particular part(s)?
    D. What are the positive aspects of perseverance?
    E. What might be some negative aspects of perseverance?

6. Consensus building:
    A. What does it mean to reach consensus about a task or part of a task before starting?
    B. Did you ever reach a consensus during the activity?
    C. If you can remember, share what this looked like and sounded like.
    D. Why might reaching consensus be important to a group?

E. When might consensus be a detriment to a group?

Variations:

- Taylor, a friend and colleague of ours, allows his building teams to rebuild a pyramid after a collapse up to where it was when it went down. For example, if the builders are lifting a pyramid that has five cups at the bottom, attempting to move in six cups, and the cups fall, the group builds up without limitations a pyramid with five cups at the base so they can make another attempt at moving in six cups. He tells us this option gives groups the motivation to build instead of waiting around for someone else to build a higher pyramid. The record for this variation, as we know right now, is a pyramid with nine cups at the base - so, a nine row pyramid.

- Require a different combination of lifters each time a bottom row is lifted.

- Allow for adjustments to be made to the cups before a lift. Anyone from the group can touch any of the cups to make them more structurally sound. Again, they can touch any cup but not lift.

- Allow for outside resources. During one interaction of the Reverse Build, Chris did not mention that outside resources could not be used. One of the building groups remembered an oversized set of cards used in a previous activity so they picked them up and incorporated them into their build. This was a valuable learning experience for this group in relation to resources - looking around to see what was possible. Now, the kinds of resources you leave around (e.g., masking tape) will be up to you.

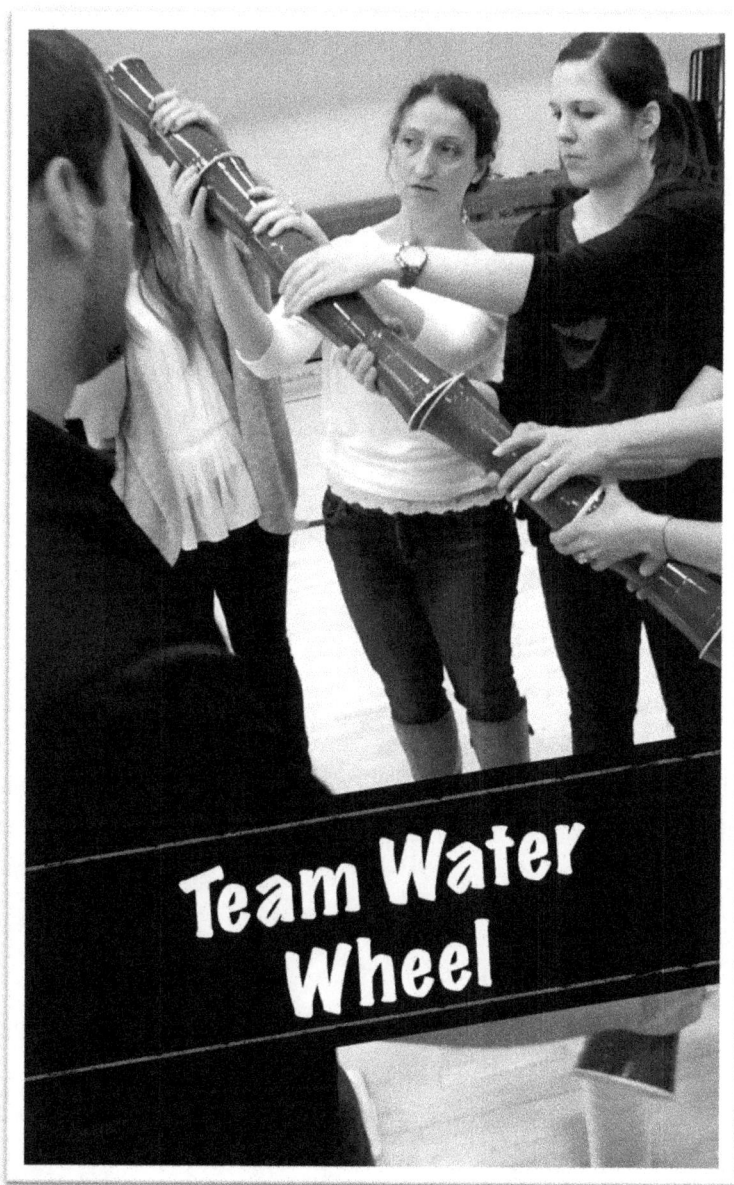

Team Water Wheel

Team Water Wheel

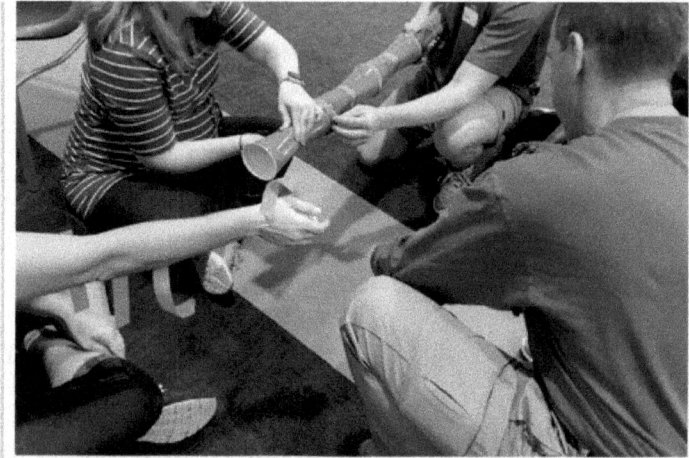

Activity Objective: This activity has two objectives. 1) How many cups can be stacked end to end supported by the team, and 2) When stacked and supported, how many times can the stack be rotated like a waterwheel in order to get as many ping pong balls into a bucket.

Facilitated Objective:
1. Measuring progress.
2. Working, collaborating with others.
3. The value of roles and responsibilities.
4. Establishing goals when you don't have all the data.
5. Discovering limits for the most effective processes.

Needs Per Group:

- 20 - 30 cups for each group of six to eight participants depending on what variation you do.

- 2 buckets

- 20 to 30 small objects, like ping pong balls or marbles.

- 1 roll of masking tape.

Numbers: Six to 40 players. Six to eight players per waterwheel group. Up to five waterwheel groups can play at one time.

Note: This is a great activity for small groups. We have found that more than eight people crowd the waterwheel a bit too much.

Time: 15 - 20 minutes.

Procedure: For those that do not know, you may need to describe a waterwheel. For example, it is a giant wheel that has buckets or paddles on the end of each arm that are moved by flowing water in a river. The water turns the wheel, which turns the axis that turns the wheel attached to a mill.

This activity consists of two rounds. The first round is to see how big of a waterwheel the group can build. The second round is to see how many objects can be carried by the wheel and dropped into a bucket.

Round 1:

One player in the (small) group will start with two cups, holding them bottom to bottom. When the cups are connected, someone else from the group will tape them together. The two cups are then rotated 180 degrees vertically like an airplane propeller (not like helicopter rotors). Each time the cups are rotated 180 degrees, the group is required to add a new cup to one end, thus seeing how big of a propeller the group can build it in six minutes.

Below are the rules for the group(s) to follow:

- Using a roll of masking tape, peel off strips no longer than your index finger one at a time.

- Use the strips of tape to secure the cups end-to-end.

- With every cup you add, you must turn the waterwheel 180 degrees. Turning the waterwheel must be in vertical motion like a airplane propeller (not like a helicopter).

- If the waterwheel breaks apart at any time, the group cannot turn the cups until the arm is fixed.

- Every player must participate in at least one of the tasks above.

- You will have six minutes to build the longest waterwheel possible.

- Time will NOT start until the first two cups are connected. (Facilitator Note: This is required so the group has time to plan before conducting the build.)

Round 2:

After the six minutes has expired for Round 1, each group has a waterwheel ready for service. During Round 1, they have also had time to practice and turn the waterwheel together as a group.

Now, place an empty bucket at one end of the waterwheel and a bucket full of light objects, like ping pong balls, at the other end. The challenge is to see how many objects the waterwheel can move from one bucket (of materials) to the other (empty bucket - at first) in three minutes.

Below are the rules for the group(s) to follow:

- Everyone must be connected to the waterwheel in some way - except for the object loader.

- Objects must be loaded in an open-faced cup (pretty much the only option).

- The waterwheel must turn 180 degrees after it is loaded.

- Once the waterwheel is turning, only a cup can carry or touch the objects.

- Objects must be unloaded (dropped into the bucket) before the waterwheel can be loaded again and turned.

- Players may not touch the objects as they come out of the waterwheel and drop into the bucket.

- If an object falls to the ground it is returned to the loading end of the wheel.

- If the waterwheel breaks apart at any time, the group cannot turn it until the arm is repaired.

- After the waterwheel is repaired two objects are removed from the bucket of earned objects to the loading end of the wheel.

Safety: When the waterwheel gets longer some groups may try to use a chair, or other object (if available) to elevate the end person so they can get high enough to rotate the wheel. Please spot this person if you allow elevation resources.

Facilitation: During our trials in creating this activity, we first tried stacking the cups without the use of tape. But all the groups we experimented with would

crush the cups and damage them. We quickly started using tape and found tremendous improvement in the treatment of the cups and overall play.

Be aware that only every other cup will have an open end for an object to be placed into. So, every other rotation will not have an object traveling to the bucket. In most cases we do allow multiple objects to be placed in a cup - often increasing the odds of objects falling to the ground.

We have found painter's tape (usually blue) works the best on the cups. It is easier than most other tapes to take off so you can reuse the cups.

When it comes to processing, we like to frontload the activity by allowing groups to come up with a goal of how many cups they can stack, and how many objects they can get into the bucket. This helps when processing at the end and comparing their goal to what actually happened.

Observations/Questions:

1. Measuring progress:
   A. How did you measure progress - by stacking the cups or the number of items placed in the bucket? Or was there some other way?
   B. Are there other variables you noticed that helped measure progress? How does measuring progress help with task completion?
   C. If the goal was stacked cups, is there anything you would have done differently?
   D. If the goal was collecting items, is there anything you would have done differently?

2. Working and collaborating with others:
   A. What do you remember about the planning phase of this activity?
   B. Did you have a particular plan in place before starting your waterwheel?
   C. Did it change during the activity?
   D. Would you say you were all collaborating, all cooperating, or a combination of both, during the activity?
   E. What are the differences between collaboration and cooperation?
   F. Why might these differences be important?
   G. What was it like for the group when the waterwheel broke?

H. How did this setback affect the task?

I. What did you do after the setback?

3. The value of roles and responsibilities:

   A. What was your role in comparison to other roles in the group?

   B. Did you feel your role was as important as others?

   C. Were there too many people doing the same thing?

   D. Why do you think so?

   E. Could you have been more efficient by reassigning roles during the activity? Explain what you are thinking.

4. Establishing goals when you don't have all the data:

   A. Was the goal you set at the beginning of the activity the same as the end result?

   B. What influenced your goal setting at the beginning when you didn't have any data to work with?

   C. What led to any differences in your results compared to your goal?

   D. How were goals adjusted during the activity?

   E. Why did you adjust your goals?

CupItUpTheBook.com - Chris Cavert & Barry W. Thompson

5. Discovering limits for the most effective processes:
    A. What limits did you discover during this task?
    B. How did these limits influence the behaviors during the task?
    C. How do you decide when you have reached a "limit"?
    D. How are limits related to success and failure?
    E. How can you use this information?

Variations:

- Another way to present this activity is in competition mode. Groups compete against each other to see how many cups they can get into their wheel in five minutes.

- Do a timed event in two rounds. The first round is to build the longest horizontal line of cups possible and the second round is to see how many rotations can be accomplished without the cups coming apart. The focus of this variation can be on the quality of the build and efficiency of the turning.

- Don't distinguish between the airplane spin (vertical turning) or helicopter spin (horizontal turning) when it comes to rotation. Let the group have that freedom.

- Instead of taping a cup to the end of the wheel before it is rotated, place an index card between the end cup and the new cup. The group then has to apply enough pressure to the waterwheel to keep the cards from falling out. If a card falls from the waterwheel, it stops. The card that fell must be placed back into its original spot before the wheel can continue to turn.

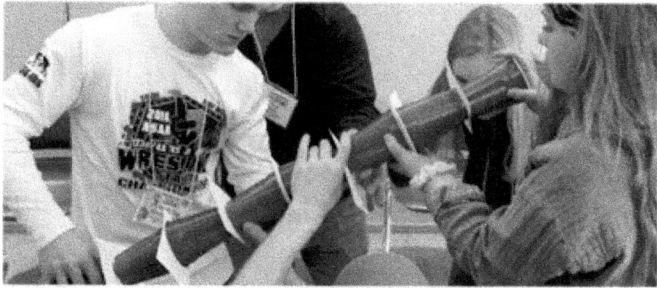

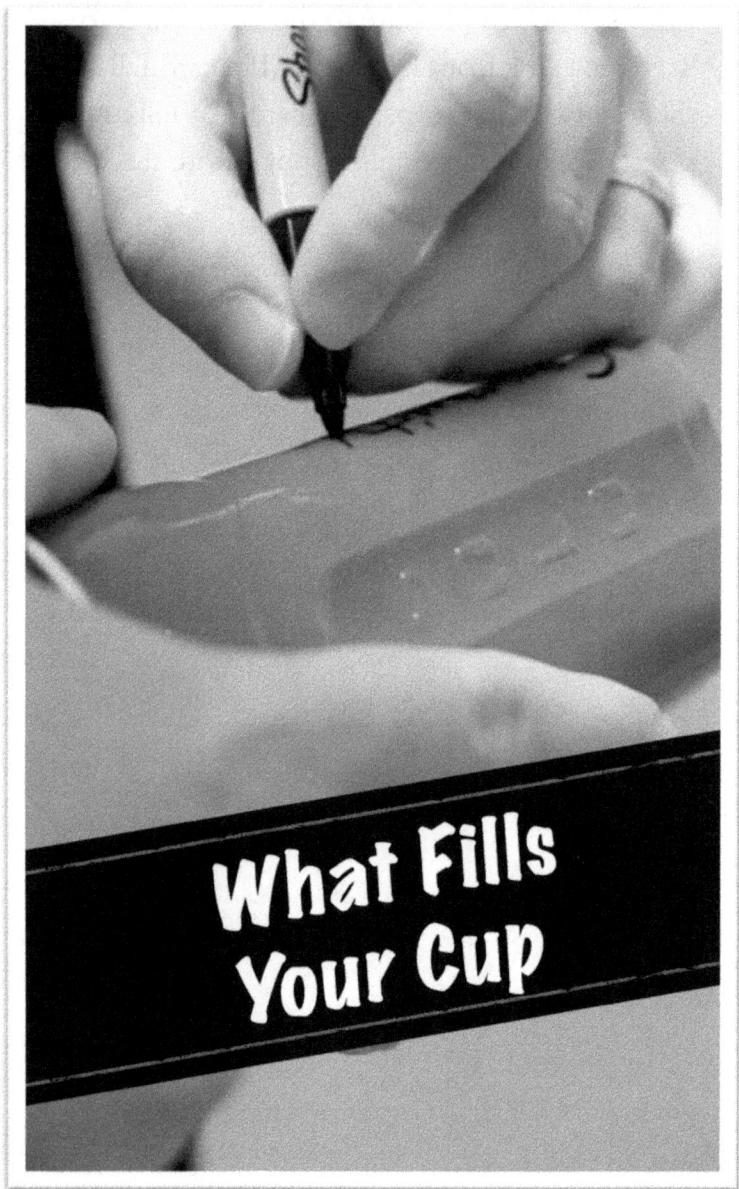

What Fills Your Cup

Discussions with Cups
What Fills Your Cup

The inspiration for What Fills Your Cup comes from the activity, That Person Over There, an ice-breaker found in The EMPTY Bag by Hammond and Cavert. Using (drawing or writing) visuals on the cups inspires creativity as well as information recall during the process.

Activity Objective: At the beginning of the program: Get to know others and ultimately remember what fills each person's cup.

Facilitated Objective:
1. Sharing information about yourself.
2. Active listening.
3. Getting to know others in the group.

Needs:
- 1 cup for every participant
- 1 permanent marker (medium tip) for every two participants (one marker for each person is optimal if you have them).

Note: We will be suggesting below that you allow participants to take their cups with them after their program, so consider the cost when you want to use this activity option.

Numbers: Works well with 10 to 50 players.

Time: 20 to 30 minutes (depending on how much information is shared).

Procedure: Each player will need a cup (when we program these activities we plan to let the players take home their personalized cup as a keepsake of the event). If you have enough permanent markers hand one out to each person. If one each is not possible, you should have a least one marker for every two people. (Pair up everyone in a fun way if they need to share the markers).

STEP 1: Ask players to write/draw three symbols on the outside of their cup (within that flat open area around the cup) that represent things that "fill" their cup. For example, things they have counted on over the years to lift their spirits, make them happy, or motivate them to "keep going!" You could stop with the directions here or provide more specifics - we have found being more specific about the symbols helps to keep the activity consistent across players.

Being more specific, ask each player to, 1) draw one (simple) geometric SHAPE that reminds them of something positive - anything that can be drawn with one single line (remember, all lines are not straight), 2) write/draw a single or two-digit NUMBER that has meaning to them, and 3) write/draw out one WORD. Again, all of these symbols should have significance to the participant in relation to what fills his or her cup.

If pairs of players are sharing a marker have them take turns - write/draw one symbol at a time then pass off the marker. While waiting for the marker players can reflect on what they have written/drawn or ponder what they will add next to their cup. When all the cups are symbolized, move on to the next step.

STEP 2: When all the cups have been prepared, ask the whole group to gather together in an open area large enough for all of them to mingle around. This will be the sharing part of the activity. Players are going to pair up. (One of the best and fastest ways we've found to pair up is to raise a hand in the air when you are ready to talk with someone else. Look for someone doing the same thing and then move together to form a pair.) It will be okay to form a group of three if there is an odd number of participants (or, you could play to even things out). Once paired, each player will take a turn to tell about what fills his or her cup - using the symbols on the cup as a visual reference.

After sharing what fills their cups, partners switch cups. When each is ready (they might want to review information) they will go off and pair up with another player in the group and tell this new person whose cup they are holding and what FILLS this person's cup - again, using the symbols as a visual reference. After both players share what's on his or her cup and who the cup belongs to they switch cups. When ready, each goes off to find another partner to talk with.

We find that this process works well for about four or five minutes. In our experience, the cognitive faculties start to wander off task after five minutes.
Warn the group that you will be stopping all conversations when there are about 30 seconds left. Warn them again when there are 10 seconds left. Then, ask them to finish the conversation they are having and move into a big circle.

When you have the group's attention ask everyone to find the person that belongs to the cup they are holding AND tell them, based on what was shared, what fills their cup. After sharing they can give the cup back to its owner. Tell the players that they might have to wait for the person they need to speak with - they might be busy talking with someone else. After each person has shared, and has his or her own cup back, they can move out from the crowd to form a large circle around those still sharing information.

As you can imagine there will be lots of interesting things to share about what happened during the activity. Once everyone is part of the circle, all with their own cup in hand, you can ask them about their experience.

Safety: Since this is a mix and mingle type of activity, there are no real physical dangers (that we have seen to this point). However, be mindful of the emotional safety of your group. We have seen (on very few occasions) players feel self-conscious about the information that gets back to them - the information was "translated" along the way forming an inaccurate picture leaving them feeling embarrassed. As always, be mindful of the readiness of your group and work out the powerful emotions right away. (Even though working through these powerful emotions can be challenging - ones we might be inclined to avoid - they often become a catalyst for meaningful learnings.)

Facilitation: During What Fills Your Cup, we often will take some time to frontload what behaviors the players might need in order to be successful with this activity. As you know, listening (more specifically, active listening) will be very important. It will also be important to be respectful about the information that is shared during the activity.

Observations/Questions:
1. Sharing information about yourself:
   A. What sorts of things fill our cups?
   B. What common "fillers" do we share as a group (e.g., parents, pets, friends, teachers, faith)?

C. Did anyone have a hard time thinking of things that fill your cup?

D. Why do you think people have a hard time thinking of fillers?

E. If a particular person fills your cup, do they know it?

F. How do you think they would feel if they knew they were important to you?

2. Active listening:

A. What were the challenges you had during the activity?

B. What strategies did you have to help you remember someone's information - about what filled their cup?

C. When your cup was returned to you how accurate was the information you heard from the person returning it?

D. What caused the information to change?

E. Does this happen at other times in your life?

F. What's important to remember about this?

3. Getting to know others in the group:

A. Would anyone be willing to share one of the symbols they added to their cup?

B. What does this represent to you?

168168

   C. What is difficult about getting to know someone? How do you overcome this - what are some of your strategies?

4. Feedback and feelings:
   A. Does anything on your cup surprise you? Why?
   B. What did you notice about your feelings while you were reading the comments?
   C. What good feelings did you recognize? What comments were related to these feelings?
   D. What negative feelings did you recognize?
   E. What comments were related to these feelings?
   F. Where do you think you get these feeling from - how did they originate?

Variations:

- If your time is limited, start by only asking the players to draw/write two symbols on their cups - what two is up to you.

- As mentioned above (a friendly reminder), each person keeps his or her own cup and writes positive encouragements and uplifting symbols for themselves. What will they remember about themselves when they look at their cup in the future?

Cup UPs!
(At the End of a Program)

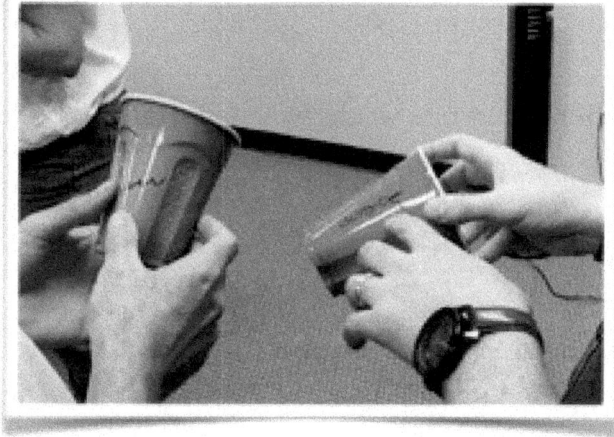

Activity Objective: At the end of a program: Leave everyone with a wide variety of positive feedback.

Facilitated Objectives:
1. Offer appropriate feedback.
2. Responding to feedback.
3. Considering positive behaviors.
4. Share opinions and values.

Needs:
- 1 cup for every player
- 1 permanent marker (medium tip) for every two players (one marker for each person is optimal if you have them).

Note: We will be suggesting below that you allow all the players to take their cups with them after their program, so consider the cost when you want to use this activity option.

Numbers: This one works well with 10 to 50 players.

Time: 20 to 30 (depending on how much information is shared).

When you are ready to present Cup UPs ask everyone in your group to find their cup (if you presented What Fills Your Cup), or you can hand out a blank cup to each person. With cup in hand, ask everyone to sit down in a circle formation. Hand out the permanent markers (one for each person or one to share between two).

You will be asking everyone to write or draw a (small) word or symbol on other player's cups. These words or symbols are meant to UPLIFT (Cup UPs) the person, as well as encourage and inspire them in the future. If you need to have the "talk" about being appropriate, please do so. Let your group know that if they cannot think of something positive to add to a person's cup, don't write or draw anything.

We like to manage the process a bit to avoid hold ups. First we ask everyone to write their first name on the INSIDE of the cup - on the top rim area so everyone knows to whom the cup belongs (if players have to share markers allow enough time for this). Then, start the passing. Have everyone pass their cup one person to the left. Say,

> "Please write or draw something uplifting on the cup in your possession. Keep your contribution small, we need to have room for everyone to share something. Do not pass along the cup to the next person until I tell you to do so."

Monitor the player's progress. Ask if anyone needs more time. When everyone is finished writing or drawing (be sure to facilitate sharing markers if needed), ask everyone to pass the cup they have one person to the left.

Continue this process of writing or drawing and passing to the left until everyone has their own cup in hand. Give the group some time to look over their cup to see what they get to take home with them. Be sure to allow some time to open up a discussion about the activity. If all goes according to plan the participants will leave with a positive anchor to their experience.

172

Safety: Cup Ups is all about providing appropriate feedback, so be sure to take some time to talk about what this looks like - in written, as well as, in verbal form. So this one is more about keeping things emotionally safe. Since the group will be sitting down during this activity, the physical safety risk is minimal.

Facilitation: If we sense that some people in the group will not provide appropriate feedback, we will, instead, ask players to write words or draw symbols on their own cups that will remind them of who they are and what they want to be. You can prompt them with: What words of encouragement do you want to remember? What behaviors do you want to keep up in your life, ones that will help you be successful? Who is a person you can go to for help?

As a keepsake, you want the cups to be something that lifts them up, something positive.

Observations/Questions:
1. Offering appropriate feedback:
   A. Is it easy or challenging to give feedback to someone?
   B. Why is this the case for you?
   C. What do you know about feedback?
   D. Is it a good thing or a bad thing for you?

E. What does it depend upon?

F. If the people in your life would be open to more feedback from you, how would this change your life?

G. If YOU would be open to more feedback, how would this change your life?

2. Responding to feedback:

A. Does anything on your cup surprise you? Why?

B. What did you notice about your feelings while you were reading the comments?

C. What good feelings did you recognize? What comments were related to these feelings?

D. What negative feelings did you recognize?

E. What comments were related to these feelings?

F. Where do you think you get these feeling from - how did they originate?

3. Considering positive behaviors:

A. What positive behaviors, things you can see and hear, do you believe are good to have when you're working within a group?

B. When these positive behaviors are present in a group, what is it like working together?

C. What is it like working within a group that is missing these positive behaviors?

4. Sharing opinions:
   A. Share some of the experiences you've had sharing your opinion about something?
   B. How do you know when it's appropriate to share your opinion? How do you know when it's right to share your opinion?
   C. How do you know when it's not appropriate to share your opinion?
   D. What choices do you have when it comes to sharing your opinion?

Variations:

- As mentioned above, each person keeps his or her own cup and writes positive encouragements and uplifting symbols for themselves. What will they remember about themselves when they look at their cup in the future? This variation can be used even if you don't have any concerns about players giving appropriate feedback to each other.

References

Tom Heck (Reference to the, *Ball, Cup, Bandana Flip* activity.) Tom Heck, "Maker, Teacher, Coach" has contributed to a wide range of educational projects and initiatives. Find links to loads of resources and ideas from technology to team building at: TomHeck.com

Sam Sikes (Reference to the, *Line 'Em Up* activity.) *When The Chips Are Down* is found in Sam's book, *Raptor and Other Team Building Activities*. It was the major inspiration for Line Em Up. Sam is the author/coauthor of eight books in the team building field. He is a master trainer, an innovative game designer and sight-after workshop presenter and speaker. Find out more at Sam's website: DoingWorks.com

Mike Spiller (Reference to the, *Line 'Em Up* activity.) I learned the activity, *Exchanging Knots* from Mike. It was another inspiration for a facet in Line 'Em Up. He has traveled the world for decades sharing, learning and collecting games and activities of all kinds. Find more than a dozen of his most popular booklets of games and activities on the Publications page at: MSGOW.com

Karl Rohnke (Reference to the, *Material Movers* activity.) The most recent write up of the team building activity *Pipeline* is found in Karl's book, *FUNN 'N GAMES* (2004). Pipeline is one of those

"move-something-from-one-point-to-another"
activities - hence the inspiration behind Material
Movers. Karl has been one of the most prolific writers
in the adventure education field - mostly known for
his activity books. Search "Karl Rohnke" on the web
to explore his epic contributions.

NBC, Minute To Win It (Reference to the, *Ping Pong
Cup Stack* activity.) <u>NBC.com</u> The challenge, *Tilt a Cup*
was played by one person on the Game Show - we
changed it to a team activity so players can work
together to bounce, catch and build the cup tower.

Dick Hammond & Chris Cavert (Reference to the
What Fills Your Cup activity.) *That Person Over There,*
found in *The EMPTY Bag: Non-Stop, No-Prop Adventure-
Based Activities for Community Building* by Hammond &
Cavert was an inspiration to a facet in What Fills Your
Cup. If you are interested in a copy of the book, find it
at: <u>TrainingWheelsGear.com</u>

Recommended Resources

Other Versatile Resources:

The Chiji Card Guidebook: A Collection of Experiential Activities and Ideas For Using Chiji Cards, by Chris Cavert & Steve Simpson. This book includes 25 different activities to program with Chiji Cards (or other picture/graphic-type cards). Find out more at: WoodNBarnes.com

Playing with a Full Deck: 52 Team Activities Using a Deck of Cards, by Michelle Cummings. The title says it all - you only need a standard deck of playing cards to lead loads of fun. Find your copy at: Training-Wheels.com

The Revised and Expanded Book of Raccoon Circles: A Facilitator's Guide to Building Unity, Community, Connection and Teamwork Through Active Learning, by Dr. Jim Cain & Dr. Tom Smith. A "raccoon circle" is a length of 1-inch tubular webbing about 15 feet long. Once you have a dozen (or so) raccoon circles and this book you can program days of team building activities. Find your copy at: Training-Wheels.com

FUNdoing.com Chris Cavert's website loading with free resources, a fresh fun-filled blog, an online store and a list of team building and training services offered by Dr. Cavert.

Whenpeopleplay.com Visit Barry's site for team building resources, training services, and blog postings for professional development and activity programming needs.

Playmeo.com One of the most comprehensive and searchable team building activity resources on the web. This subscription-based service has over 250 activities with full descriptions, printable directions and videos of play (for most entries). And, continues to grow. Free activities available.

Training-Wheels.com The most comprehensive online store for team building resources - books, activity gear and processing props. You will also find a subscription-based activity database and informative blog.

BONUS MATERIAL! If you would like an easy download of the instructions and questions to the activities in this book, then please visit: http://www.fundoing.com/resources.html

or

As a thank you, we want to give some bonuses for buying the paperback. To get your bonuses please visit http://www.whenpeopleplay.com/cup-bonus

About the Authors

Dr. Chris Cavert is an internationally known trainer
and speaker and a past recipient of the Association for
Experiential Education's Karl Rohnke creativity award.
He has been working experientially with groups of all
ages for more than 25 years.

Chris is the author of over a dozen books related to
activity-based experiential group development. He
holds an undergraduate degree in physical education, a
master's degree in Experiential Education and an
educational doctorate in Curriculum & Instruction.

As an educator Chris focuses his lessons on how to use team building activities to develop pro-social skills within groups of all ages and build strong and resilient communities.

Chris currently resides in Denver, Colorado. He loves hiking and camping in the mountains, walking long beaches and good chocolate!

You can contact Chris via:
Email: chris.cavert@gmail.com
Twitter: @ChrisCavert
Website: FUNdoing.com

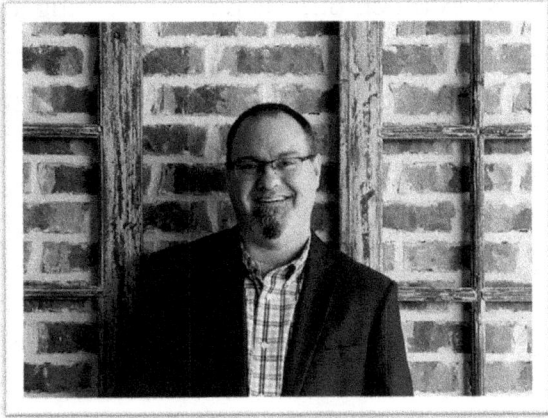

Barry [W] Thompson, For the last 26 years Barry has been educating, training and speaking to groups about how to become high performing teams. His hope and vision is to encourage others to see the power of using experiential adventure-based education to facilitate growth in their own circles.

Currently, Barry owns and operates WhenPeoplePlay. Dedicated to help build a better work culture. Facilitated team building to connect, grow and develop organizations. Working with corporate and non-profit groups to help with communication. He specializes in experiential activities to build trust and teach the importance of conflict, commitment, and accountability.

Barry spends as much time as possible writing about personal development, team development, leadership, and of course, games and activities that bring out these traits in a fun and engaging ways.

Barry currently resides outside of Dallas, Texas with his wife, Lori and two Shih-Tzus - Buddy and Chase. He enjoys disc golf, drawing, and reading whenever he has some time to spare.

You can contact Barry via:
Email: barry@whenpeopleplay.com
Twitter @BarryWThompson
Facebook www.facebook.com/whenpeopleplay
Websites: Whenpeopleplay.com for more games, videos and resources.